A simple country girl arouses the passions of the king and is brought to his capital, showered with luxury and subjected to the wiles of the world's most practiced seducer. Yet, even though sometimes tempted, she remains true to the shepherd she has loved since childhood. She rejects the worldly riches offered by the king, and returns to her first love and a joyous future of fulfilment.

This is the story Dr. Bob Dryburgh brings out of the Song of Solomon, which, he leads the reader to understand, is also the story of what every Christian faces when worldly temptations entice him away from his love for his own Shepherd.

Fascinating in its scholarship, exciting in its drama and inspiring in its revelation of God's purpose displayed in human love, *Lessons for Lovers in the Song of Solomon* is a book to be cherished by all who have loved.

Lessons For Lovers in The Song of Solomon

BOB DRYBURGH

Keats Publishing, Inc. New Canaan, Connecticut

LESSONS FOR LOVERS IN THE
SONG OF SOLOMON

A PIVOT BOOK

Pivot edition published 1975

Library of Congress Catalog Card Number: 75-7807

Printed in the United States of America

PIVOT BOOKS are published by Keats Publishing, Inc.
36 Grove Street, New Canaan, Connecticut 06840, U.S.A.

CONTENTS

PREFACE

Throughout the Bible we sense God's anticipation that those who get to know Him will become "lovers of God" (2 Timothy 3:4). Many of the principles on which love for the Lord operates on a very practical level have been hidden in the Song of Solomon by the Holy Spirit.

The Shulamite's love is very much like our own. It burns brightly, flickers a little, then flares again when least expected. The shepherd shows a constant love that does not change. He is not affected by circumstance. He moves, acts, and trusts with one motive—to bring joy and peace to the woman he loves.

I have looked for the personal message of the Song; the message that ties the heart of man to the heart of God. It is a vital message; one that is easily missed and often avoided. Throughout the study, I have had in my mind the echo of the Lord's own words: "If a man love me . . ." (John 14:23).

Bob Dryburgh

Chapter 1

DON'T COMPROMISE
YOUR LOVE

The girl of Shunem had lived a sheltered life. Her brothers dominated the scene in her single-parent home, forcing her to do a man's work for long hours each day, but she did not fight it. Taught love by her mother, she had learned to care for the lambs and kids of the flock with personal tenderness. The grape harvest gave her a sense of fullfilment also, since she had been left with the full responsibility of the vineyards. Her long, almost endless hours of work helped provide the family with a stable, though small, income.

Every growing thing interested her; the budding pomegranates, the lilies in the valley, the foxes in the bush. She knew the sound of every singing bird that echoed through the valleys. The call of the dove, separated from her mate, particularly fascinated her. She knew how the little bird felt. She was in love too. Her shepherd beloved had to spend weeks away at a time on the distant pasture land.

They were betrothed and would marry soon. She remembered how her mother had pledged her to the shepherd in the outdoor ceremony, underneath the apple tree. It had been the happiest day of her life. There was just no one like her shepherd; a great lover, patient, tender, so different from her brothers.

The valley was his favorite place. He enjoyed the pasture there for his sheep, liked the flowers, admired her vineyard, and really enjoyed the pomegranates. She interrupted her reverie. Why not visit the nut garden in the valley now? The vine should be checked for new growth, and there might be some budding of the pomegranates. She moved quickly along the familiar paths until she came to the crest of the hill. Starting down into the valley, she caught her breath as she looked across the familiar landscape, green with the fresh life of spring. To her, it was the most beautiful place in the world.

Suddenly she saw the men, strangers to her world! She ran! They chased and caught her. Terrified, she listened as they told her that they were the king's men, that Solomon had seen her, and that he now desired her to come for an audience with him. They did not hurt her, and promised that they would not. Gradually, the trembling and fear subsided. The men were acting on the imperial command, she told herself, but she could hardly believe what they were saying, that Solomon thought her the most beautiful of women, and wished to speak with her in the palace.

She prepared to go. Hurriedly she gathered her few dress items together. Her pulse raced as she washed, dressed, and walked to the waiting carriage, attended as never before in her rustic life.

The trip to Jerusalem was filled with anticipation. Could this really be happening? What would the king be like as a person? Was she really as beautiful as the men had said? She wondered how long she would be away from home. How excited her friends would be to hear what had happened to her!

The carriage drew up before the palace grounds. She was stunned by the splendor of it all. Every tree was cultured to perfection; every bush shaped to enhance its surroundings. The flowers stretched in an endless profusion of multicolored beds in every direction.

She was greeted courteously by a member of the palace staff, and quickly taken into one of the majestic residences. The attendants knew exactly what to do with her. They began to prepare her to meet the king in accord with his wishes alone. No one asked her how she would like to dress, what perfume she preferred, or how they should do her hair. Her room, her bath, her clothes, and her spikenard perfume, were all the choice of the king.

The preparations are completed hastily. Without delay, she is taken into the presence of King Solomon. The attendants retire, and the king begins to speak with her as a man to the woman he loves. Aware that she is appealing in his eyes, the Shulamite feels more pert and beautiful than ever before in her life. The king's charm has a strange effect on her that she has never had to cope with before. It is at once exhilarating and frightening.

Solomon proposes to the Shulamite. She cannot believe what she is hearing. Again he offers her the desired place by his side, bride of the king of Israel. In this role she would have great status in the society of Jerusalem. Unlimited possessions would be hers for the asking; clothing, jewelery, perfumes. Serving men and women would be responsible for her comfort, seeking to enhance her beauty that she might remain appealing to the king. No mention was made by Solomon of the other wives, or of the numerous concubines.

Solomon's proposal swept beyond all the wide ranging exploits of the Shulamite's wildest fancies. Like a mighty tidal wave, it roared through her soul, pushing her to forget the past, let go of all commitments, and begin to live on a new horizon of discovery and experience.

The king waited for her response. The model of simplicity and charm, his whole bearing said that nothing of all he possessed meant as much to him as the girl from Shunem.

Tempted beyond all reason to accept his invitation, the Shulamite knew that she had to mention her betrothal to the shepherd. How could she tell the king about this without losing everything? She began to plan a compromise, and said:

> *"Let him kiss me with the kisses of his mouth: for thy love is better than wine"*
> (Song of Solomon 1:2).

Three people are involved in her answer. She is the speaker. "Let him kiss me . . ." refers to the absent shepherd. "Thy love is better . . ." is spoken directly to the king.

The Shulamite is telling Solomon that his love, as well as his offer, is intensely desirable, but that because of an earlier promise to the shepherd, she was bound to at least fulfil some of the terms of her engagement. Her total lack of sophistication shows in that she even made such a suggestion. She is under extreme pressure in a totally strange set of circumstances, feeling the total authority and absolute power of the king.

The Shulamite had made her pledge to the shepherd because she did fervently love him. She loved him enough at the time to wish that he might spend the rest of his life with her. Her depth of feeling when betrothed does not show when she says to the king, "Let him kiss me . . . ," as though his right to kiss his bride must rest on the whim of the king. Her love has cooled since the moment of commitment by dint of circumstance.

The compromising Christian has the same problem. His love has cooled. Any commitment to the Lord becomes weak and soon takes second place to his prominent interest. Though willing to compromise, he still wants some kind of relationship with the Lord. Just as Solomon could recognize her cooling toward the shepherd, Satan, the tempter, knows our spiritual temperature. It is he alone who is the alternate choice to the Lord Jesus Christ. He soon dominates the heart that has slipped away from the love control of the Lord.

The Christian of every age feels the pressure to compromise. By shading the truth slightly, the businessman has the opportunity to obtain a larger order. The fun-oriented teenager feels that a total response to Jesus Christ will take the zest out of living. The young executive anticipates a quicker climb if he adopts the social behaviour of his superiors.

Even in Christian service this may be true. The singer feels he will have a wider ministry if he sings some of the world's songs. The teenagers' sponsor becomes very popular by advocating extensive social and sport activity and short devotionals. The preacher is tempted to minimize some phases of Bible truth not pleasing to his congregation.

"We are not ignorant of his devices," said Paul in his letter to Corinth. The Christian must develop an awareness to the trappings Satan builds around the compromise situation. The opportunity seems to be a fleeting one. It feels as if there will be loss if he does not follow through. Excitement and advancement are often involved. The natural man desires it. The hidden barb is missing while the decision is being made. Immediate pleasure often accompanies compromise, but like all the pleasures of sin, it will only last "for a season" (Heb. 11:25).

The Shulamite recognizes that there is a difference between her feeling for the shepherd and the response she feels toward Solomon. This creeps into her conversation with the king.

"Because of the savour of thy good ointments thy name is as ointment poured forth, therefore do the virgins love thee" (Song of Solomon 1:3).

Solomon smelled good. This was most attractive to the girls because bathing facilities were not always readily accessible. When Solomon's name was mentioned, it was immediately associated with

the fragrant perfumes that were so important to
him, and thus characteristic of the man.

One of Christ's followers poured a pound of
spikenard on His feet. As a result, the whole house
was filled with the aroma of spikenard. Spikenard
was one of Solomon's favorites. The spices on his
body gave a pleasant aroma which reached all who
were near him. It was because of this fragrance
that Solomon was so appealing to the young
women of Israel.

Love based on the smell of a person's body
must be very superficial indeed, yet this is the level
on which Solomon's romances functioned. It was
for this kind of love that the Shulamite began to
consider passing up her commitment to her shepherd beloved to become one of the women in Solomon's harem. Solomon and his things had begun to
fascinate her to the point that her judgment was
blurred.

Two loves now exist in her life instead of one.
She no longer has a clear distinction between right
and wrong to guide her. The king senses that she is
trying to evaluate her feelings, and that she has
placed a value on his affection for her.

The Bible teaches that if we compromise as
Christians, we will have a new love in our lives
which will compete with our love for the Lord
Jesus Christ. It is easy to settle for enjoying the
things we can see and touch, but when we do, the
invisible Lord slips completely out of our focus,
and before long we hardly miss Him.

Since our interest is then drawn to a sinful
world, we soon begin to lose the sharp good-evil
contrast. Everything becomes relative. The importance of the will of God lessens as we become con-

fident of our ability to judge for ourselves what is
best to do in any situation. We are often completely unaware that our spiritual vision has
blurred.

Still compromising, we try to make our two
loves exist side by side, forgetting that true
love requires submission, and that the Lord taught
that, "No man can serve two masters. . . . Ye cannot serve God and mammon" (Matthew 6:24).
Compromising in our Christian lives will never
clear up the conflict. It will only add to it.

The drama of the Song took place in a world
where hot and cold running water was unknown.
Bathing was a real project in the cold season, so
the common man would try to make up for his lack
of cleanliness by the use of fragrances within his
budget.

Solomon was different. Attendants prepared
his bath, cared for his personal grooming, and
maintained an abundant supply of exotic perfumes
and skin creams. This made him very alluring to
the young women. They "liked" him, for this is the
meaning of the Hebrew word.

The Shulamite mentions only the externals
about Solomon as appealing. No inward qualities
of the man drew the girls into his harem. His personal interest in any one of them was, of necessity,
fleeting. His lusting heart craved new and different
conquests. He was willing to settle for simply being
"liked" by his many wives and concubines to
achieve his goal.

Satan fits this picture. There is nothing attractive to us in him as a person. We know that his
aims are all evil, even corrupt. He personifies everything we know about wickedness, lust, guile, and

depravity, yet when he appeals to our hearts we find it easy to respond. Something in us likes the things he offers.

Our true love response to the Lord Jesus is at once jeopardized because of this. The real joys of living through each day with Him become lost. Many of us are settling for less than the Lord wants to give. Our attention caught by the devil's games and toys, we live weak, disappointing, failing lives, and wonder how it ever happened.

In contrast, by yielding ourselves to the Lord, we can experience the fulness of living with Christ every hour while we share in His great work of changing lives, aware always of the warmth and power of His great love.

The Shulamite continues her course of compromise. This will mean she settles for a far different relationship with the shepherd than he planned for her at the time of betrothal. She talks to the king as he takes her into his personal chambers.

> *"Draw me, we will run after thee: the*
> *king hath brought me into his chambers:*
> *we will be glad and rejoice in thee, we*
> *will remember thy love more than wine:*
> *the upright love thee"* (Song of Solomon
> 1:4).

She does not intend to repudiate Solomon completely. The enchantment of this man obscures his evil plan from her thoughts. She will accept him because he is king over the kingdom where she lives. She will allow him to control part of her life.

The great mistake she makes is that she includes the shepherd in her design of compromise.

When she says, "Draw me, we will run. . . ," she is wrong. The shepherd could only see Solomon as an enemy bent on destroying the human relationship most precious to him. The more the king "drew" the girl away from him, the less motivation the shepherd would feel to ever run after Solomon. Loss of his lover would be no less hurtful because she was won by a king.

The Lord Jesus is our true Beloved. If we decide to let Satan dominate a part of our lives, we go against the wishes of the Lord. He is not bound to share with us the experiences of life where we act contrary to His will.

The disciples of Christ had been called by Him to fish for men. After Jesus died, Peter decided to go fishing for fish again, taking several of the other disciples with him. Time after time, they let down the nets only to draw them in empty. Dawn was breaking when Jesus appeared on the beach.

"Children, have ye any meat?" He called to them.

He knew the answer would be "No!" but desired to rivet in their minds the truth that any activity of life, outside of His will for them, would be empty and fruitless.

"Cast the net on the other side of the ship," He called. What could possibly be the difference? The water was the same on both sides. The difference was that now they lowered the nets for Him, at His command. He was partner with them in the work. The nets were loaded to the limit when they pulled them ashore.

The Shulamite had learned to trust the shepherd to the point that she expected him to be faithful in every circumstance. Yet, as she said, "Draw me," to Solomon, she was denying her true beloved where it would hurt him most. He could not go along with her in this.

There was nothing in Solomon to attract the shepherd, just as there is nothing in Satan to attract the Lord Jesus. They stand apart. Jesus crystallized this truth one day, saying, "The prince of this world cometh, and hath nothing in me" (John 14:30). There was no area of response in the Son of God to anything the evil one could offer, do, or say.

Solomon takes the Shulamite at her word. She asks him to draw her, so he leads her into his private apartment. She is now faced with seduction by the enemy who does not look like an enemy even at close range.

She next speaks about being glad, even rejoicing, in Solomon. Up until now, the shepherd has been the source of her joy. Being near him has made her want to dance and sing. The shepherd's closeness had made the days seem bright and full of promise. He had stirred her, for this is what the words literally mean. The stirring of her emotions is now committed to Solomon, and the naive girl expects the shepherd to go along with this.

A deep, continuing, inner joy is built into the Christian who is in love with Jesus Christ, Son of God. Compromise soon spoils all this. While still going through the outward acts of Christian living, the compromiser begins to feel a sense of duty or necessity pushing him through his paces. The surge of total surrender rising from true devotion is gone. He has begun to drag his feet spiritually, and he may not know it yet.

The Shulamite and the shepherd had built some memories during their courtship that were uniquely precious to them as a couple. Places and people had special significance to them because of shared experiences. A whispered word or phrase could set off a whole emotional reaction.

Now she is ready to make a complete shift as she says, "We will remember thy love more than wine." Present adventure is future memory. In her mind, the decision has already begun to form that the excitement in the rest of her life would be built around Solomon. She has not yet fully comprehended that her whole future relationship with the shepherd is in jeopardy, for she still uses the plural: "We will remember . . ."

Her repeated reference to wine reminds us that in her time, water in the populated centres was often polluted and dangerous to drink. Wine was considered the safe and healthful beverage. She rationalizes that Solomon's love is good for her. It would have been easy for her to go on to say that the king had brought into her life new dimensions of interest, experience, and knowledge that she could not otherwise have known.

That is how Eve thought in the Garden of Eden. The forbidden fruit looked extremely desirable. There was promise of fulfilment—knowing more—although the record points out that all she gained was a knowledge of evil. She had already been taught the good. Her decision cost her the loss of a precious relationship with God.

Almost as an afterthought, she adds, "The upright love thee."

Solomon was a popular king with large segments of the nation Israel. His reign was marked with peace, so the country prospered without the expense of war. He built the temple in Jerusalem, planned by God, and revealed to David in detail. Capable of great wisdom, Solomon wrote and published many profound sayings that were widely accepted and quoted. Even when he grew old and corrupt, taxing the people mercilessly, they remembered the good days, failing to see that he no longer practised the wisdom he was teaching. They liked him, and this was noticed by the Shulamite.

Her comment comes close to the contemporary expression, "Everybody does it!" so often used when there is no reasonable or Scriptural explanation for an action. There is a great spiritual hazard in ever using this as our standard of behaviour.

Even in times when God moves in power among His people, there is always a segment of the Christian community that follows far behind. Worse still, in periods of spiritual departure whole congregations will abandon His standards while still claiming to be servants of the Lord.

During the latter years of Eli the priest, God's people accepted a custom that was in total violation of the Divine law. Samuel wrote about it years later. God had commanded that when an offering was given to Him, all of the fat of the sacrificed animal belonged to Him. The priests could share some of the meat of certain offerings. "The priest's custom was, that, when any man offered sacrifice, the priest's servant came, while the flesh was in seething, with a fleshhook of three teeth in his hand; and he stuck it into the pan, or kettle, or caldron, or pot; all that the fleshhook brought up the priest took for himself" (1 Samuel 2:13-14).

This custom made no allowance for the fat to be given to the Lord.

Once in a while, a worshipper would mention this, and would be openly ridiculed for holding to the old fashioned ways. Samuel tells how force was used to make some people accept this custom. From the leaders down, God's people had adopted the practice of disobedience. It was not right, but everybody did it.

Paul the apostle wrote to Timothy about how Christians should act. He did not suggest that Timothy check around the various churches, strike an average of the church members' habits, then live that average. He pointed Timothy to the inspired writings. These were the basis on which his future behaviour must be charted. The true servant of God must be controlled by God alone and His standard is outlined in His Word.

The Shulamite had not comprehended yet that it was the will of the shepherd, and his desires, that must shape her life. Looking around her at the responses of "the upright," she was almost ready to compromise the greatest love she would ever know right out of her life.

Chapter 2

BE WILLING
TO BE DIFFERENT

The interview with Solomon was terminated by the king. Attendants took the Shulamite to the residence of the king's women. As she entered the palatial apartment complex, she became aware that she was being closely watched by all the women present. Every eye followed her as she moved.

To the cultured, sophisticated daughters of Jerusalem, she was an unusual person. Her outdoor activities had tanned her skin to dark perfection. Her body was supple, yet firm and strong. She exuded health and athletic vitality so lacking to the indoor, pampered types commonly associated with the court.

Looking around the others, she realizes at once that she will always be a stranger to these women. They were a different breed than she had ever known. Immediately she becomes self-conscious about her skin, feeling that this is what makes everyone stare. She wishes inwardly that she looked more like they did. To those who were near she said:

> *"I am black, but comely, O ye daughters of Jerusalem, as the tents of Kedar, as the curtains of Solomon"* (Song of Solomon 1:5).

There was a difference between the girl from Shunem and the daughters of Jerusalem—and it showed! She was not trying to be different. She was different. She would have preferred, at least for that moment, to be just one of the crowd, alike in appearance with the rest of them.

Every Christian needs to discover that he is distinctly different from the person outside of Jesus Christ. He does not have to work at it. The very moment he receives Christ as Saviour, the Holy Spirit builds into him a new nature, with new appetites, desires, and interests. He is inwardly changed from the person he was before conversion to a new creature in Christ.

The apostle Paul became so excited about this truth that he declared, "Therefore if any man be in Christ, he is a new creature: old things are passed away; behold all things are become new" (2 Corinthians 5:17).

It is God alone who makes the Christian different. The change is not simply the result of a new environment as he seeks out Christian friends. Nor is it psychological in nature; a tranquility resulting from confession of sins.

God builds the difference right into his person.

He is changed on the inside. God has always done this with His people. Moses taught centuries ago, "The Lord doth put a difference between the Egyptians and Israel" (Exodus 11:7). True believers in the Lord Jesus become "partakers of the divine nature" (2 Peter 1:4), and can never be the same again.

The Shulamite was not one of the daughters of Jerusalem, but she was tempted to become as like them as possible. To do this she had to turn from her shepherd betrothed so that she could embrace the king as they did. Skin colour had nothing to do with it. Turning away from the shepherd proved to be very hard for her, particularly since she knew he was alive and loving her wherever he was. His unchanging love set her apart, putting her in a different category from the others. His love held her steady when she was weak.

The God who makes the Christian a different person is willing to maintain that difference, not only as an inward quality, but also in the outward demonstration of the power and presence of an indwelling God.

You are not expected to live the Christian life on your own initiative, nor in your own strength. The Lord has more than just a beginning to give you. He will gladly enable you to express the new life you have received if you will only let Him do it.

The Bible teaches: "If, when we were enemies, we were reconciled to God by the death of his Son, much more, being reconciled, we shall be saved by his life" (Romans 5:10). The Shepherd of your soul is alive. His love is poured into your heart by the Holy Spirit. He is willing to unfold His plan for your life to you as you respond to His love. He will then live in you, and through you, the wonderful life He wants you to have.

Just as His death for you was perfect, so His life through you will be perfect. Your part in all of this is so to love and trust Him that you will let Him make it happen.

Although the new girl was deeply tanned, her beauty and appeal were not diminished. In her simple country way, she says, "I am black, but comely:" black like the tents of Kedar, comely like the beautiful curtains of Solomon. The Hebrew word for "comely" means more than superficial beauty. It contains the idea of beauty in the home. She knew that she was pleasant to be with. Two men desired her. Her choice would place her beauty in a tent, like the tents of Kedar, or in the richly furnished rooms of Solomon's palace.

The outward signs of the inward change are what make you attractive as a Christian. If you are spiritually alive, you now have spiritual sight which is the counterpart of your natural sight. By faith you can focus your spiritual eyes on Christ and as soon as you do a wonderful promise of God becomes operative: "But we all, with open face beholding as in a glass the glory of the Lord, are changed into the same image from glory to glory, even as by the Spirit of the Lord" (2 Corinthians 3:18). The Lord is able to develop in you a likeness to Himself by His Spirit. The world may reject this image—may even try to mar and spoil it.

Even when men oppose you, they will recognize that what God has wrought in you has resulted in true beauty in human character.

> *"Look not upon me, because I am black,*
> *because the sun hath looked upon me: my*
> *mother's children were angry with me;*
> *they made me the keeper of the*
> *vineyards; but mine own vineyard have*
> *I not kept"* (Song of Solomon 1:6).

Happy to have her beauty noticed, the Shulamite wanted her difference to remain in the background. Compromise is still in her mind. This is what makes the difference a problem to her. She explains that she has been scorched by the sun, and leaves the implication that the tan will not last. She was not always like this and will not always remain so tanned.

She then refers to the circumstances of her home life. Since she was the low member on the family totem pole, she had much work forced upon her, and could not look after herself or her things as she would like to have done. The very qualities that made her attractive to the shepherd she now discounts and wishes to minimize.

Her whole reaction is like that of a Christian who has just made some worldly friends and wants to please them. The compromise comes close to denying the Lord, and may go just that far.

Look closely at Peter standing within the high priest's house. He is warming himself at the fire of the Lord's enemies. One man hears him speak and recognizes that his dialect is different from the others. He lifts his hand and points the disciple out, saying, "Of a truth this fellow also was with him: for he is a Galilean" (Luke 22:59).

Without the least hesitation, Peter reacts: "Man, I know not what thou sayest." What had begun so simply had slipped into an identification with the enemies of Christ, and isolation from the Master. Peter had denied his Lord.

The Shulamite does not go to the point of denying the shepherd. However, as she reaches for the approval of those who are not his friends, her interest in the things that please him diminishes. She is moving, however slowly, toward rejecting him.

Chapter 3

KEEP IN TOUCH

Solomon tries everything to make the Shulamite feel at home. It is important to him that she
relax and drop her guard, he wants her to feel that
he is a true friend.

He ordered that she should be given the care
of some kids from the royal flock. In the shepherd
culture, girls cared for the very young of the flocks.
She had done it at home. Now Solomon planned to
make her feel at home by engaging her in the same
activity, so that the strange new environment
would be less frightening to her. It is most likely
that she was tending her little flock when she saw
the shepherd, or heard his voice. Instantly she was
aware of his love that brought him so great a distance to be near her. We cannot know whether he
had brought his flock across the mountains, fields
and roads, or whether he was engaged for a time

with another flock, but he was near to her in her time of need; this was all-important to him.

"Tell me, O thou whom my soul loveth, where thou feedest, where thou makest thy flock to rest at noon: for why should I be as one that turneth aside by the flocks of thy companions?" (Song of Solomon 1:7).

The Shulamite's heart stirred at his presence as it had so often done before. In the morning, with much to do, and with other shepherds active close by, he could not be seen alone with her, but she did speak to him, asking directions. Unable to embrace, she spoke so that only he could hear, "O thou whom my soul loveth."

While her eyes had sparkled at the breathtaking richness of the palace, and her unsettled heart had calculated how much her beloved's love would cost her, there was no question that her soul, her inmost person, responded only to the shepherd. He was her great love. She loved him with her soul.

To know the depth of the Shulamite's love we need to understand the soul; what it is, and how it functions. The Scriptures get very definite in this area of truth, and claim to be able to separate between soul and spirit "for the word of God is quick, and powerful, and sharper than any two-edged sword, piercing even to the dividing asunder of soul and spirit, and of the joints and marrow, and is a discerner of the thoughts and intents of the heart" (Hebrews 4:12).

The rich farmer, spoken of by the Lord, had reaped a great harvest. Concerned over storage

space, "he thought within himself saying, 'what
shall I do ...'?" Still talking to himself he said,
"so, thou hast much goods laid up for many years;
take thine ease, eat, drink, and be merry" (Luke
12:17-19). When he talked with himself, he talked
with his soul. The soul, therefore, must be the self,
the real you.

In contrast to the soul, the spirit is that part
of a man that is dead before conversion, and which
experiences regeneration when the sinner trusts the
Lord Jesus for salvation. Jesus singles out the
spirit of man when He speaks of the new birth:
"that which is born of the Spirit is spirit" (John
3:6). When the Holy Spirit goes to work to change
a man for eternity, He brings the dead human spirit through the process of re-birth, to the experience
of new life in Christ.

After a person has become a Christian, he has
an avenue of communication with God that was
not there before. The Bible explains this: "the
spirit itself beareth witness with our spirit ..."
(Romans 8:16). He does this because He wants
to get a message through to the real self, the soul.
It is this experience of the Spirit speaking, through
the spirit, to the soul, that John refers to in his epistle. "He that believeth on the son of God hath
the witness in himself" (1 John 5:10), says John,
knowing so well that the unbeliever does not have
this channel of communication operative. The witness is not in the spirit, but in the soul, the real
self. It is simply through the spirit that the channel
exists which carries the message to the soul.

Before this salvation experience, all the messages to the soul come via the senses of the body.
These messages are still sent to the soul after con-

version. This causes a conflict. The old nature, through the body, makes many demands for gratification. The Holy Spirit opposes and keeps on presenting the will of God by way of the re-born human spirit.

The conflict must be resolved in the soul. First, the incoming information will be assessed intellectually. Second, there will be an emotional reaction to it, for the great emotions are experienced by the soul. Third, your response of the will must settle the direction you will take for yourself. The soul, the real self, decides to respond to the appeal of the flesh through the physical senses, or to the appeal of the Holy Spirit through the senses of the human spirit.

While Solomon presented many physical attractions, it was the shepherd who was loved by the soul of the Shulamite, by her real self. At least, that is what she claimed.

Speaking to His disciples in the upper room, just before going to the cross, Jesus said, "if a man love me, he will keep my words" (John 14:23). It is not enough to say that I love the Lord Jesus Christ with all my soul. The real evidence for love is found in the life I live, and in my personal response to His will for me.

The uncertain responses of the girl might cause us to question whether her profession of love was sincere. It is important to know that just before she spoke about her love she had said, "Tell me ..." There was a link between the love in her soul for the shepherd, and his spoken word. She required information from him to guide her in the steps she must take.

As a Christian, you need to know the will of

your Beloved, as revealed in His Word, so that you might express your love through action, in response to the Lord's directive. This was lived by the Psalmist who taught: "Thou art my portion, O Lord" (Psalm 119:57). The evidence that this was real with him is shown by what follows; "I have said that I would keep thy words. . . . I thought on my ways, and turned my feet unto thy testimonies. I made haste, and delayed not to keep thy commandments" (Psalm 119:57, 59-60).

The Shulamite needed to know two things. "Where thou feedest . . ." this was the shepherd in action. The location changed daily as the individual flocks were taken to different areas for feeding. He was providing his flock with food. "Where thou makest thy flock to rest at noon." At the time of greatest heat, the flock would be kept at rest. He also would rest, and would find time and opportunity to speak with her.

It became intensely important to her to know where he would be, because she needed to talk with him. The result of not knowing would be a search for him when she should be resting. She explains her reason for asking. "Why should I be as one that turneth aside. . . ?" or as the revisers put it, "as one that is veiled. . . ?"

The harlots, with their veils on, would wander through the resting shepherds looking for a man. It seems intolerable to her to even create the appearance of such behaviour. She is really saying, "why should I wander?" knowing well that the word of her beloved, if received, believed, and acted upon in faith, would save her from wandering and endless searching.

The children of Israel had known God's great

salvation from Egypt, had passed through the Red
Sea, and had heard Miriam's salvation song as their
enemies perished in the waters. Camping on the
very fringe of the promised land, they sent twelve
spies into the land to give an eye-witness report to
the Israelites. Each of the spies on returning veri-
fied the Lord's description of abundance in the land
flowing with milk and honey. They brought back
one cluster of grapes so big that two men carried it
between them. They also reported that the men in
the land were strong, vigorous, and huge in comparison to God's people.

The tragedy of Kadesh-barnea took place
when ten of the twelve spies claimed that the children of Israel could never wrest the land from the
powerful nations inhabiting it. Only two of them
saw the victory that could be theirs if they simply
claimed the promise of God who had given them
the land by covenant. Caleb and Joshua knew that
God's strength, not theirs, could give them the
land.

The people rejected the Word of God that
day, and began forty years of wandering. The
Scripture tells us that, "the Lord's anger was
kindled against Israel, and he made them wander in
the wilderness forty years . . ." (Numbers 32:13).
Wandering is the only alternative to claiming the
promises of Scripture by faith.

To avoid wandering, the Shulamite needed to
receive the word from the shepherd personally. He
was the one who could tell her what she needed to
know right then.

This is the way the sons of Korah felt when
they were experiencing revival. They knew that
while the Lord had been speaking, they had not

been listening. No personal word from him had reached them while their love was chilled. Now they cry out individually, "I will hear what God the Lord will speak" (Psalm 85:8). No longer did they think of Him as a distant God, removed from their day-by-day lives. He was now "God, the Lord" to them. Their heart response to the Lord as Lord made it imperative that they hear what He was saying. There would be no wandering when they walked under His control. Their complete confidence in His ability to instruct them showed in their concluding words, "and shall set us in the way of his steps" (Psalm 85:13).

Listening to the shepherd, the Shulamite believed every word he said. She knew him well enough to trust him, but more than that, she had inwardly resolved to act on the words he was saying. These words could keep her from wandering, and while this would satisfy her own need, she also knew that her response would bring joy to her beloved.

Peter speaks of the Lord Jesus Christ as the "Shepherd and Bishop" of our souls. He is the only One who can tell us what we need to know to keep from wandering. Our response is a source of joy to Him as He explained through John to Gaius, "thou walkest in the truth. I have no greater joy than to hear that my children walk in truth" (3 John 3-4).

> *"If thou know not, O thou fairest among women, go thy way forth by the footsteps of the flock, and feed thy kids beside the shepherds' tents* (Song of Solomon" 1:8).

Just as the Shulamite had spoken aside in gentle tones that no one else could hear, "O thou whom my soul loveth," so the shepherd in his answer returns, "O thou fairest among women." This had nothing to do with the instructions for which she had asked. It was a reflection of his heart in words.

To all others she was tanned and dark, even swarthy. In her own eyes, she was "black, but comely." To the shepherd, she was fair—"fairest among women."

The word he uses suggests a brightness akin to a shining light. It cannot refer to her dark outward appearance, although that is beautiful. There is an inner brightness of purity which he values, recognized only by himself, and this makes her very precious to him. Her total outward expression carried the reflection of the inner beauty as she spoke her words of need to him.

The Lord desires to see "truth in the inward parts" (Psalm 51:6). Paul had a struggle to weld together his heart's desire to please God, and the ultimate experience of spiritual victory. His assurance of pleasing the Lord as he found his way through problems lay in his secret passion: "I delight in the law of God after the inward man" (Romans 7:22). He was building up his hidden inward man with the living Word of the Eternal God. This would keep on living within him, and doing its great work of holding him steady while it strengthened him for every area of his life and ministry. The impact of the Word upon his heart would be felt in time of temptation to deviate from the will of God, first, in giving the needed correction and direction, and then in empowering him to take the course he knew to be right.

To the woman he considers most beautiful of all, the shepherd's instructions are basic. If she did not know where he was, she must do two things. Firstly, she should follow where the flocks had gone. Secondly, she should pasture her kids near the tents of the shepherds. These two simple steps would enable them to find each other.

If she followed the footsteps of the flock, she would be following those who had followed him, and would ultimately find him in the place of leadership. By finding the shepherds' tents, she would find those who were like her beloved—shepherds— and he would be among those who were like him.

If you long for a closer fellowship with the Lord, find exciting instruction in these words. Look for those who are following the Lord. Have your close friendships with them, not with the worldly crowd, or with the wandering Christians, who have no direction to their lives. Then look for Christ in other believers. Discover those through whom His love flows to the world around. Share with them in their times of Bible-study and prayer. Join in their outreach, as they care for those with needs and hungers, pointing them to Christ. As you remain close to the people who love the Lord with a pure heart, the Holy Spirit can bring the reality they have into your life.

The Thessalonian Christians illustrate this principle. They received the Word of the Lord in much affliction, although it afterward brought them joy. This Divine Word caused them to follow men who in turn followed Christ. Paul writes: "ye know what manner of men we were among you for your sake. And ye became followers of us, and of the Lord, having received the word . . ." (1 Thessalonians 1:5-6). Note that the eventual outcome of this was that they found the faith of the men they followed, and thus became followers of the Lord. Paul re-enforces this truth as he later writes to the Corinthians, "be ye followers of me," he says, "even as I also am of Christ" (1 Corinthians 11:1).

The Shulamite had only to follow the shepherd's instructions if she wanted to see him during the day. The faithful shepherd lover would do his part if she would respond to his words.

Similarly, the Lord will make His presence known to us if we are obedient to Him. Thomas was getting more confused by the minute as Jesus described His departure to His disciples. Mixed up and disturbed, he said, "Lord, we know not whither thou goest; and how can we know the way?" (John 14:5).

Jesus looked at him and said, "I am the way" (John 14:6). He was more perplexed than ever. His fluttering heart steadied a little when Jesus finally said, "I will not leave you comfortless: I will come to you" (John 14:18).

Later on the Lord spelled out how it would work. If His disciples would obey His instructions, He would not only be near them, but He would make them aware of His nearness. "He that hath my commandments, and keepeth them, he it is that loveth me: and he that loveth me shall be loved of my Father, and I will love him, and will manifest myself to him" (John 14:21).

The girl was alone during the morning, but she knew that as the noon-time drew near, her shepherd beloved was moving toward the same spot as

she. They would meet, for the promise was sure
and definite, though not spelled out in words. For
us, James gives the word: "draw nigh to God, and
he will draw nigh to you" (James 4:8). As we follow the plan of approach he gives, we can be confi-
dent that our Shepherd moves to meet us for the
joy of fellowship and love. Contact is assured.

Chapter 4

HOW DO YOU COMPARE?

The curtain opens once more bringing the golden splendor of the royal dining-room into view. Servants flit to and fro with busy dignity in the twinkling light of flickering oil lamps. The finest food in the world, exquisitely prepared, served in delicately formed gold and silver dishes, invites the guests to partake with joy. The king shares the table with her, but the girl from Shunem has lost her appetite.

Snatches of the table conversation reach us, as Solomon uses the same love phrases that trapped so many other girls. The Shulamite is unmoved. Another voice is speaking to her heart as she remembers her time with the shepherd to whom she is betrothed. Oblivious to the king, she thinks of the person of her true beloved, and of the joy of sharing with him, while the king prattles on, comparing her to horses.

> *"I have compared thee, O my love, to a*
> *company of horses in Pharaoh's chariots.*
> *Thy cheeks are comely with rows of*
> *jewels, thy neck with chains of gold. We*
> *will make thee borders of gold, with studs*
> *of silver"* (Song of Solomon 1:9-11).

The horses in Solomon's chariots were not ordinary horses. Their discipline was perfect; their movement beautiful. Every hair in the mane and tail was brushed to a glowing lustre. The most ingenious workmanship in gold, silver, and costly gems adorned the bridle, the collar, and every part of the harness as the team moved with rhythmic precision. The breath-taking majesty of it all made the watcher forget that it was beauty from a land and a people who cared nothing for the God of Israel.

God had no part in the desire Solomon had for the Shulamite. Solomon's flesh lusted for what his eyes saw. To him, she was an object to be possessed and enjoyed for his own gratification, without regard as to whether her needs would be met or not. He could never give her what she really needed in a man because he had already committed himself to so many others. Yet, every time he mentions her beauty he speaks of adding to it.

The necessary trappings had to be added to make the horses work together. Her cheeks were comely to him, "with rows of jewels." The beauty of her neck is linked to the "chains of gold." He assures her that he will add even more to all this glitter: "We will make thee borders of gold, with studs of silver."

The king, who could never satisfy her longing

heart, offers to add ornaments to her make-up that will not improve her. The jewelry was simply his investment in a method of seduction that had, no doubt, worked many times. He wanted her to look greater in her own eyes. The trinkets, however costly, would not add to her appeal to the shepherd, but rather stood as a threat to her own continuing purity, and to the shepherd's future enjoyment with her of the real fellowship of love.

> *"While the King sitteth at his table, my spikenard sendeth forth the smell thereof. A bundle of myrrh is my well-beloved unto me; he shall lie all night betwixt my breasts. My beloved is unto me as a cluster of camphire in the vineyards of Engedi. Behold, thou art fair, my love; behold, thou art fair; thou hast doves' eyes"*
> (Song of Solomon 1:12-15).

During the meal, she remembers the words of her true beloved, spoken when they were together: "behold, thou art fair, my love; behold, thou art fair; thou hast doves' eyes." She recognizes the shepherd's love to be a selfless love. He loves her for who she is, not for what she can give or do. His love keeps on giving, not taking. The words of the shepherd never suggest that he will make her more beautiful, or that she stands in need of such improvement. His love sees a perfection in her that is hidden from the king.

The remembered conversation is precious to the Shulamite. The words are consistent with the language of the shepherd throughout the story but do not fit Solomon's conversation pattern. It was the reality of the love evidenced in the conversation that strengthened and stirred her heart against the overwhelming temptation. The shepherd had mentioned doves. The doves in Palestine were a species that migrated annually, were of value for sacrifice to the Lord, and mated with another of the species for life. The commonest type has an unusual wailing sound, and is thought to mourn for its mate in his absence. When alone, the one thing the dove longs for is the sight of its mate. The shepherd had recognized in the eyes of the Shulamite this hunger, this longing for him alone, and her answering joy at being with him.

No wonder the girl could not enjoy the feast at the king's table. The inner turmoil was building. Her heart, that had once responded to true love alone, was now exploring another kind of love, where the criteria lay in the stimulation of the physical senses alone, rather than in the interaction of two hearts.

The Lord Jesus speaks of the love which He expects to draw from our hearts. To emphasize His teaching, He draws an extreme comparison, saying, "if any man come to me, and hate not his father, and mother, and wife, and children, and brethren, and sisters, yea, and his own life also, he cannot be my disciple" (Luke 14:26). The love that the Christian will have to the Lord, when he really knows Him, will be so great that the other loves in his life will seem like hatred by comparison.

This is the love that the Holy Spirit puts into our hearts. It is the "love of God" (Romans 5:5). God has the ability to enter a man, and so possess him, that He will enable the creature He has formed to love as his Creator loves. He then di-

rects the flow of that love back to the God who
gave him that capacity to love in the first place.

Deeper than the most intense human emotion,
this love shows itself in total involvement with the
Lord. Represented in the New Testament by the
Greek word, agape, it represents a total response of
the heart to the person loved, based on the discovery of hidden values in the person not seen by others. The person loved becomes so precious to the
lover that he is no longer thought of as an object
of pleasure. Rather he is prized for what he is. So
completely absorbed does the lover become in this
love that he sees the other person as intensely
worthy. He becomes sacrificial in the demonstration of his love. He would die for the loved one.

In his Expository Dictionary of New Testament words, Vine says that agape is "the characteristic word of Christianity . . . the Spirit of
revelation has used it to express ideas previously
unknown." The greatest demonstration of the love
the Lord looks for in our hearts is seen as He offers
Himself on the cross at Calvary for our sins—"Who
loved—agapao—me, and gave Himself for me"
(Galatians 2:20).

The Holy Spirit portrays this love for us in
the Song of Solomon by contrasting the best and
purest in human love, with the sensual physical attraction between two bodies.

The Christian who loves the Lord Jesus with
this spirit-implanted love has eyes like the dove,
looking always for the Lord, longing for Him, and
watching for evidence of His presence in daily personal experience. He values the shepherd who loves
him, knowing that he is not worthy of so great a
love.

Like the bride, he looks at the trinkets of the world, and sees them as worthless, aware that they will only come between him and the lover of his soul. He knows that the Lord loves the inward beauty of the cleansed and surrendered heart, and strives to have this to present to Him. Valuing the sound of his Beloved's voice, he spends time with God's Word so that he might really understand what the will of the Lord is. He will remember these words as the Shulamite did, and they will hold him steady in a time of temptation.

Our appetite for the things of the world is spoiled when we learn the joy of the Lord's love. Like the girl from Shunem, drawn by so many enticements, we discover that when the reality of the world's pleasures is within our reach, these pleasures no longer look good. The variety, from a distance, looks to be infinite, but John sums up in total everything that is there when he says: "For all that is in the world, the lust of the flesh, and the lust of the eyes, and the pride of life, is not of the Father, but is of the world. And the world passeth away, and the lust thereof" (1 John 2:16-17).

The offer Satan made sounded tremendous to Eve in the garden of Eden. The lust in her eyes responded to the forbidden fruit. Her flesh lusted after the new taste, because it was, "good for food" (Genesis 3:6). She listened to his assurance that they would be like gods, and pride within her surged after the idea of becoming wise. The appeal of the world hit her on three levels, and she collapsed. All she really got out of it was a moment of sweetness in the mouth. It cost her a lifetime of heartache and sorrow.

Although she was not enjoying her dinner with

the perfumed king, the Shulamite had lost something in coming to the feast. She says, "While the King sitteth at his table, my spikenard sendeth forth the smell thereof." A girl like her would not normally wear spikenard. Imported from India, spikenard was extremely costly, and consequently was found only on the bodies of the rich. Likely, her attendants, as one of the final touches in preparing the Shulamite for supper, applied the spikenard to her body to please the king. As the new aroma enveloped her, her normal fragrance, which would likely be myrrh, known and loved by the shepherd, was lost.

There is a fragrance that the Lord desires to find associated with the Christian. Paul refers to it as he writes to the Corinthians: "Now thanks be unto God, which always causeth us to triumph in Christ, and maketh manifest the savour (or fragrance) of his knowledge by us in every place" (2 Corinthians 2:14). This fragrance, associated with knowing the Lord, enters the Christian, and can so shape him inwardly that the invisible fragrance, lost on the unknowing world, becomes visible or "manifest" in the total impact of the life he lives. Paul completes the declaration that he himself has come to preach the Gospel, and then continues his theme: "For we are unto God a sweet savour of Christ, in them that are saved, and in them that perish: To the one we are the savour of death unto death; and to the other the savour of life unto life" (2 Corinthians 2:15-16).

Notice that it is the fragrance of our lives as we witness. The sweet fragrance rises from us as we share Christ with other Christians and they become willing for death to sin. It rises as we share

Him with the lost and our witness brings them to eternal life in Christ.

The Shulamite sits at Solomon's table with a new fragrance which an evil king has brought into her life and which can bring no pleasure to the shepherd, reflecting as it does another world where he does not belong, and in which he can have no part.

The Christian who responds to the invitations of Satan will lose his fragrance. In simple terms, this means that he will cease to be an effective witness for Christ. He will not be able to preach crucifixion of the old man, because other believers will see the contradiction of his preaching in the life he lives. "How shall we, that are dead to sin, live any longer therein?" (Romans 6:2). The unconverted will not see in him the difference that knowing Christ can bring about, since he will not be "making manifest the fragrance of his knowledge" (2 Corinthians 2:14), but will rather be living close to the level of the man without Christ.

The person who shares the fleeting temptations of the world's table does so at Satan's request, and will not carry on his person the fragrance of Christ as he rises from that table.

Even while she sits with Solomon, the girl thinks of her beloved and compares him to, "a bundle of myrrh," and, "a cluster of camphire." These were likely the perfumes she normally wore, since they come from plants readily available to her, and would cost little.

Myrrh was obtained by piercing or cutting the bark of a particular type of Balsam tree, and gathering the exuded resin. Becoming hard on exposure to the air, the reddish coloured myrrh, shaped like tear drops, has a pleasing aroma. In the past it was very valuable in countries of the east where the trees did not grow.

The wounding of the tree, the tear shape of the droplets, and the bitter taste, have combined to cause some students to see suffering symbolised by myrrh. The Shulamite would likely wear some of the hard drops of myrrh in a little pouch hanging from her neck, and would leave it in place all night long.

If you know the Lord, you should have continuously within your heart an appreciation of the sufferings of Christ upon the Cross. Your life will become fragrant for God because of the influence these thoughts have upon your heart.

Our Shepherd wants to remain close to us, held near in our deepest affections. For this reason, He left us the loaf of bread and the cup of wine, saying, "This do in remembrance of me" (Luke 22:19). He knew how easy it would be for us to forget His sufferings, so He prepared a memorial. As we eat of the bread, that broken loaf reminds us of His body which hung upon the cross, with every bone out of joint. As we drink of the wine, we remember that it was His own blood that was poured out at Calvary because He loved us.

Paul suffered greatly in his service for Christ. Out of a heart that loved he gave everything he had to his Beloved, never complaining about the abuse he personally experienced as the Good News was scattered to the peoples of the world. His great hunger was to "know Him." Part of knowing Him for Paul was what he called "the fellowship of His sufferings" (Philippians 3:10), so that he might be made conformable to the death of the Saviour he loved. He was sure that a real understanding of the sufferings of the Lord Jesus would have a profound influence on every part of his personal life.

The bundle of myrrh was in the bosom of the Shulamite, just as the sufferings of Christ will have a special place in our heart's affections if we truly understand and appreciate the cost of our redemption.

The girl also compares her beloved to, "a cluster of camphire." Camphire is usually called the henna-flower, and is found in abundance on the west coast of the Dead Sea, at a place called Engedi. The henna-flowers are small, mostly white, and very fragrant with a pleasing perfume. Though they are very common in Engedi, they are not tolerated in the vineyard by careful husbandmen as they sap the strength of the land. They grow to six feet in height. The vineyard is the place for vines, not huge flowering shrubs.

The Shulamite's beloved had come into her ordinary struggling life, bringing into it a fragrance and a beauty that gave it meaning and dimension, immeasurable by the standards of the world. To her it was like a beautiful, ever so fragrant bouquet of henna-flowers, discovered in the businesslike atmosphere of a vineyard, possibly with the burly farmers still at work.

Deeper truths lie hidden in the meanings of the words used by the Shulamite. The word "camphire," means a cover. It can refer to a ransom, a satisfaction, a sum of money, or a redemption price, according to Strong's Concordance. In Hebrew, it comes from the root of the word "atonement." She mentions a cluster of henna-flowers. A great cluster of blessings are found in the atoning work of Christ: forgiveness, justification, reconciliation, righteousness, salvation, peace with God, to name a few.

Engedi means "fountain of a kid," and the word for "kid" comes from a root word meaning to cut off. Often in the Old Testament the kid of the goats was used for a sin offering. This pointed to the death of the Lord Jesus Christ on the cross, where He was "cut off, but not for Himself" (Daniel 9:26).

You grow as a Christian when you appreciate the suffering and death of Jesus Christ. You mature quickly as you go on to understand the many facets of His atoning work. The Lord will mean more and more to you as you appreciate the wonders of His atonement on a deeper level.

The Shulamite uses the same descriptive words for the beloved as he had spoken earlier, "Behold, thou art fair." What he had seen in her was really a duplication or reflection of his most precious quality—an inward beauty based on truth, known, and practised. There was no contradiction between what he seemed to be, and what he was.

She adds one new word in her description of the shepherd: "pleasant." The true meaning of the word is delightful, or full of delight. It suggests that to her, the shepherd was always exciting to be with. There was never anything stale about their relationship. Each new discovery she made in him was pleasant to her. She could grow to know him with the assurance that what she had yet to learn about him would only add to the joy she had in him that already overflowed.

This is how it is with the Lord. David knew it would be hard to explain, but he tried. "Delight thyself also in the Lord," he said, "and he shall give thee the desires of thine heart" (Psalm 37:4).

The final words of the first chapter were spoken in the palace by a girl whose heart was in the country.

> *"Behold, thou art fair, my beloved, yea,*
> *pleasant: also our bed is green. The beams*
> *of our house are cedar, and our rafters of*
> *fir"* (Song of Solomon 1:16–17).

She was speaking to herself. Surrounded by the refined, cultured, artificial beauty of both craftsmen and artists, she remembers how green the pastures were with the giant cedars and the fragrant fir trees. Even though the palace has its appeal to her, she knows inwardly that this is not her place. Neither city nor palace please her. Like a tender flower in the valley, she has grown up in the gentle quietness of a rural setting. She thinks of the shepherd tent with its grass floor, a bed made of the surrounding greenery, and the trees of Lebanon arching over with their protecting branches. This could only again be hers if she returned to her shepherd.

The fragrance of the cedar floating through the tent would be forever gone, replaced by the sophisticated perfumes of the palace crowd, if she surrendered to the wishes of the king. Although away from the shepherd's fellowship, she still speaks with him in mind as she refers to "our bed," "our house," and, "our rafters." She is identifying with him in heart while she is in fellowship with those who consider him a person with no significance or importance.

Meanwhile the shepherd is alone. The fellowship he desires with her has been taken from him. He knows how poorly equipped she is to stand against such overwhelming temptation, so his heart aches for the girl he loves.

The holy Spirit draws a picture of the Christian who is not walking in close fellowship with the Lord, but who still considers himself to be on the Lord's side. He will fellowship with those who walk in darkness, on their terms, and in the midst of sinful pursuits, although he may draw a line as to how far he will go. The truth is, he does not belong there. The Lord calls, "Come out from among them, and be ye separate . . ." adding the promise, "I will receive you" (2 Corinthians 6:17).

Chapter 5

LET YOUR FEELINGS SHOW

One of Solomon's possessions was located in a valley near the mountains of Bether. From the windows of the valley residence, the mountains could be seen so near that the rough cliffs and crags were easy to identify. It seems as if some of the king's wives and concubines lived from time to time in the country palace.

Bethabara, the "Bethany beyond Jordan," is considered by some to be the geographic site of it, since it is the city that best fits the descriptive material of the Song.

The Shulamite's journey from Jerusalem was made over a rough winding road. The rugged terrain near the Bether range forced them to worm their way down the wall of each ravine, only to bottom and begin again the crisscross climb for the top of the next ridge. Rain, and the changing temperature exposed the large rocks in the ancient

53

roadbed, making the carriage plunge and roll as it moved along the rutted road to the rhythmic beat of the horses' hooves.

The girl wondered about the days ahead. Life in the palace had been a drastic culture shock to her. Solomon decided that the country residence was the place where she should stay. She could have a portion of the vineyard for her very own. There were trees, flowers in abundance, and nature lore everywhere for her to enjoy. Besides, he introduced her to the novelty of fox puppies, personalizing them as a gift from her king. He felt sure that they would win her gentle heart, causing her to forget the past, as they cavorted, tumbled and played.

It may have been while she walked the gardens of the king's estate that the Shulamite said,

> *"I am the rose of Sharon, and the lily*
> *of the valleys"* (Song of Solomon 2:1).

All around her were beautiful, cultured flowers, produced by the world's greatest gardeners—a rainbow display of perfectly formed petals. She remembers the small flowers that gave her joy as she watched the sheep, and names two of them. The Rose of Sharon has generally been thought to be the Narcissus, a meadow flower that grows in great profusion on the Sharon plains. The lily of the valley, another wild flower, has a simple beauty that appealed to the Lord Jesus. He mentioned the lily in His preaching. The scarlet-purple colour made Him think of the robes of Solomon, but the Lord decided that the lily, or anemone, had it over Solomon for eye appeal.

These were the commonest flowers in the

fields. They must have seemed insignificant compared to the blooms in Solomon's garden, but in a burst of self-realization, the Shulamite sees herself in the wild flowers of the pastures and fields.

They grew among rugged surroundings filled with many enemies, just as she had. It was God, not man, who supervised their growth, and provided for it. In return, the little flowers became a blessing to those who had little or nothing by this world's standards. The tiny flowers had no strength of their own but had a beauty that showed, and a scent that was uniquely their own. They made the wilderness places attractive and pleasant.

Paul could see himself as "less than the least of all saints" (Ephesians 3:8), and called on others to walk as Christians, "with all lowliness and meekness" (Ephesians 4:2). He recognized the tremendous benefit of seeing ourselves as we are. Paul saw himself as the greatest of sinners, and the least of saints, so God was able to take him up and use him for His glory. Paul had already come to grips with the truth that he had nothing of himself to glory in.

It was the Lord who made Paul such a powerful evangelist. Paul could never have become this by doing his best. The Lord accomplished it through the man who knew he had done his worst, but that God still loved him, and would use him if he remained bowed in spirit at the feet of the Son of God. Instead of trying to do a great work, Paul had to concentrate on one thing, getting to know the Lord better. God will demonstrate how powerful He is in the life that is yielded, with love plus nothing, to Him. He looks for loving surrender in every Christian.

Joy springs to the Shulamite's heart as she thinks how her shepherd beloved had once compared her to all the other girls he had known:

"As the lily among thorns, so is my love among the daughters" (Song of Solomon 2:2).

His heart of love valued her gentle beauty so much that all of the others by comparison, appeared coarse and unappealing to him. He responded to her alone.

The lily has no thorns in its supporting stem. Thorns would have to be on other plants surrounding the little flower. A lily among lilies would not be specially noticed, but a lily alone among thorns would be a stand out! The thorn is associated with the curse of sin. God had said to Adam long before, "Cursed is the ground for thy sake; . . . Thorns also and thistles shall it bring forth to thee . . ." (Genesis 3:17–18). It is vital that the Christian allow the Lord to remove the evidence of the sin curse from his life. Jesus moved among sinners, with love flowing from His heart toward them, yet He was "holy, harmless, undefiled, separate from sinners . . ." (Hebrews 7:26).

The completed work of salvation, with the inward ministry of the Holy Spirit, helps us to be aware of our nothingness apart from Christ. Salvation also beautifies us in the eyes of the Lord. This is the beauty that makes the Christian like the lily among thorns to His Beloved. The Lord looks deeper than the skin of man to see the inner beauty of likeness to Himself.

The beloved's description tells of another

value he sees in the Shulamite. Though he sees her as beautiful in unattractive surroundings, he notes the thorns as well as the lily. They pose a threat to her. He can visualize the thorns with no lily present.

The Lord told a parable in which good seed fell among thorns, and although there was life, the thorns "sprung up and choked them" (Matthew 13:7). He identified the thorns definitely as, "the care of this world, and the deceitfulness of riches" (Matthew 13:22).

Before the enticing king had ever reached from his throne to try to steal the Shulamite from him, the shepherd had considered himself her protector. It is significant that the thorns in the parable of the New Testament tie in so closely with the very temptations that were thrown in the pathway of the Shulamite—the care for the world and the seduction of its riches.

Scanning the grounds, she now looks for something with which her shepherd can be compared. Erect, tall, strong, he is like a tree—but not just any tree. He is like the apple tree, with its delicious and nourishing fruit.

> "*As the apple tree among the trees of the wood, so is my beloved among the sons. I sat down under his shadow with great delight, and his fruit was sweet to my taste*" (Song of Solomon 2:3).

It was the fruit that made the difference between the apple tree and the other trees. The shepherd beloved was different in his interaction with her than any other man had been. Others might have protected her as he had done, spreading his covering arms like the spreading branches of a tree, so that even when she did not know where he was, she knew that her care was his great concern. He did more. He nourished her, meeting the needs of her heart in a way that none other had ever been able to do. When she was with him, she had the ability to live and walk in a way that would have been impossible without him. He brought out the best in her—helped her to her full potential.

Only the Lord Jesus Christ so loves and satisfies the Christian. The portrayal of the apple tree, or perhaps the citron tree since it is the common fruit tree of the region, refers in detail to what the Lord Jesus becomes to the Christian who loves Him.

"I sat down." Sitting down pictures the rest we find in Christ, but we must sit down. It is possible for us to rest on Christ for eternal salvation, while we struggle hard to make our daily salvation work. We know that it is disastrous to try to work for eternal salvation. As lost sinners we discovered that nothing we could do would be sufficient to pay our debt to God. When Paul said, "not of works" (Ephesians 2:9), he was amplifying the message declared by the lips of the Saviour while He hung on the cross at Calvary, "It is finished" (John 19:30). The work of salvation was completed by the Saviour when He died on Golgotha, and the sinner appropriates the benefits by faith alone. Otherwise he misses the joy of salvation entirely, only to wonder for an eternity of judgment how he could have missed a provision that was so complete, and so freely offered.

Daily salvation must be appropriated by faith

as well. We must believe that God knows what He wants to do in our lives. Then we must make ourselves available to Him so that He can do it. Our rest grows from our understanding that the work of God must be done by God alone, although He will often work through human instruments to accomplish it. Even as we take upon ourselves the yoke of the Lord to work for Him, we must acknowledge several things. Firstly, the strength for the work must come from the Lord. Secondly, the direction for all action must be given by the Lord. Thirdly, the timing for its fulfilment must be the result of the Lord's programming, not ours. "It is God which worketh in you," says Paul, "both to will and to do of His good pleasure" (Philippians 2:13). The key to acceptable service lies in this text.

Jesus dealt with this in His teaching. He said, "Take my yoke upon you, and learn of me; for I am meek and lowly in heart: and ye shall find rest unto your souls" (Matthew 11:29). The yoke is now being worn by the Son of God. He is already moving with it. His great strength has proved sufficient for the work. As the Christian fits the other half of the yoke to his own shoulders, he must know at the outset that his strength is not needed to move the yoke forward. He has but to walk with Jesus and the task will be completed. He will find rest in his soul as he walks.

This rest is missed when we consider the work of the Lord as something we must try our hardest to perform. Paul tells us that this is not the way of the Lord. "Faithful is he that calleth you," he explains, "who also will do it" (1 Thessalonians 5:24). The work to which the Lord calls us must be done by the Lord. We are just instruments, privileged to be in the Master's hand, as He does His work.

In the Bible we are encouraged to enter this rest by believing, in contrast to the Israelites who died in the wilderness because they would not believe. They knew that powerful giants occupied the promised land, and thought they had to depend on their own ability to beat the giants.

One characteristic of the man who knows God's rest is that he has "ceased from his own works" (Hebrews 4:10), just as God ceased working, and rested on the seventh day. In this spiritual rest, God takes possession of our bodies, and uses us to do things that had previously been beyond our reach, even though we had tried our hardest to please God.

The Shulamite remembers sitting down to rest "under his shadow." We find rest in nearness to the Lord Jesus Christ, with His shadow, the evidence of His presence, falling over us. Protected from the elements and powers against us, we have the Lord hovering over, for this is included in the root meaning of the Hebrew word for shadow.

Isaiah pictures a weary land, uninterrupted by hills, barren and waste, without vegetation under foot. The traveller becomes dazed and worn by the sheer continuity of it. Suddenly, a great rock is seen on the horizon. He struggles toward it, finally stepping out of the rays of the blazing sun, into its welcome shadow. Isaiah goes on to tell of the Man who is like the shadow of a great rock, no matter how weary the land is.

The Man is the Lord Jesus Christ. To those who have found their rest in Him, He is "as the shadow of a great rock in a weary land" (Isaiah 32:2). Remaining close to the Lord is our key concern. It is here that we will be resting and producing at the same time. The abundant life is lived close to the Lord.

The apple tree was not mobile. It stands as a reminder that the Lord Jesus does not change His position. Just as the Shulamite could not have the shepherd and Solomon, the Christian is faced with conditions on which fellowship with Christ are possible. He must come to where the Lord is, having the disciple heart, willing to obey the Word as it is gradually unfolded to him by the Holy Spirit. The Lord's holiness requires that we come with all sin confessed and forgiven.

David asks: "Who shall ascend into the hill of the Lord? or who shall stand in his holy place?" (Psalm 24:3). We could paraphrase the question: "Who will come near to the Lord, and who will stay close to Him?"

David explains that four essentials are required. Firstly, we must have clean hands. This cannot mean that our hands have never sinned, but rather that they have been cleansed from the sins committed, by confession to God, and the resulting Divine forgiveness. Secondly, we must have a pure heart, with no plans in it for future sinning. Thirdly, we must not lift up our souls to vanity. Our dedication must not be to any temporal pursuit or goal. We must be giving ourselves to the Lord for His use. There is no emptiness or vanity in this. Fourthly, we must not have sworn deceitfully, failing to keep the vows we made earlier to the Lord. We give what we have promised to the Lord.

The blessing of the Lord is assured if we follow this approach. David makes this clear when he says, "He shall receive the blessing from the Lord" (Psalm 24:5).

The bride came to where the beloved stood, and found rest with his shadow upon her. While the Lord Jesus cannot change His standards to make it easier for us to draw near to Him, He does give assurance that if we will approach Him on His terms, His presence will be with us. We will share "great delight" with Him.

"His fruit was sweet to my taste," exclaims the Shulamite. Everything he did was pleasant and acceptable to her. At no time did he offend or disappoint, since his actions were motivated by a pure, though intense love. His words satisfied her inward hunger, assuring her of her place in his heart. There had been a completeness in what they shared, with nothing missing that he could have given at that time.

The spiritual taste buds of a born-again person are pre-set to find their delight in the Lord Jesus Christ. His works and words will always thrill us if we keep on tasting of them, but we must never forget that taste is present tense. Just as yesterday's food cannot now be tasted, yesterday's spiritual food has already been built into the inner man. We require spiritual delights which we are now tasting.

"His fruit was sweet. . . ," says the Shulamite, but even as she says it, she knows that it is only the memory that is with her. She is missing the taste of new delights in him. It is the activity of the Beloved to-day, and what He says to the heart to-day, that gives abundant joy and aliveness to each hour.

It was "his fruit" that blessed the Shulamite. No matter how widely we may read in the writings of others about the Lord, our "great delight" will come from the teaching we receive directly from Him. We need Him to lead us through His Word. This will keep us from leaving the way of truth. We will then know where to go, and what to do, because He has taught us.

This is demonstrated in the life of Paul. Newly converted, and with so much to learn, Paul spent much time alone with the Lord who had promised, "I will show him . . ." (Acts 9:16).

Years later, Paul speaks about this time. "I conferred not with flesh and blood," he writes, "but I went into Arabia, and returned again unto Damascus. Then after three years I went up to Jerusalem to see Peter, and abode with him fifteen days" (Galatians 1:16-18). Paul came to the Lord alone for instruction and thus set the pattern for his life. The joy of having the Master build the Word into his understanding made him continue coming to Him for more. Gradually the truths of the church became clear, and he spent years teaching them to others. Paul never forgot how important it was to learn from the Lord Himself, and how essential for spiritual maturity. Paul claimed authority in his teaching, saying, "he made known unto me the mystery" (Ephesians 3:3).

We need to come directly to the Scriptures each day, to receive the Word by communion with the Lord. He will apply it to our hearts as well as introducing it to our minds. After we have found the message for our hearts, we can compare what He has taught us with other Christian's findings. The Word will still remain sweet to us then as it did to the Psalmist who could say, "Thou hast taught me. How sweet are thy words unto my taste!" (Psalm 119:102-103).

The manna was sweet as the children of Israel received it from the Lord. It was just right for their taste. The Lord made sure of that. After a while, they became more sophisticated in their handling of it. They began to work it over in the mill or mortar, or they would bake it in the oven. As a result, "the taste of it was as the taste of" fresh oil (Numbers 11:8). The sweetness was gone. No matter what other form of instruction the Christian receives, he must receive teaching directly from the Lord if the Word is to remain sweet to him.

Food gives strength to our bodies, but His food gives strength to our spirits. This soon shows as a spiritual vigour which manifests itself in activity. The Lord who builds the strength within us is willing to direct the movement as we start to walk. He knows where He wants to take us. The Shulamite was willing to walk in the direction of the shepherd's choice, and remembers the occasion.

"He brought me to the banqueting house, and his banner over me was love" (Song of Solomon 2:4).

The banqueting house, or house of wine, to which they had walked was likely no more than a vine arbour near the wine press where they had shared lunch and conversation together. Solomon spread a canopy, or banner, over the special guests at his banquet in the palace. The shepherd had covered her with something infinitely more precious, though invisible to the human eye. It had been as though a bower of love had arched above them, identifying them completely with each other for a time, making the simplest, most commonplace actions become tokens of their great devotion to each other.

The most exciting memories we cherish often sound so simple in telling that they are never mentioned except to our Beloved. The quiet hour alone with the Lord, when He invades the heart with the warm vitality of His great love, may be the memory link that binds my affections forever to Him.

The Lord brings us to these experiences when we are ready and willing. There is a definite order in the Shulamite's response. She draws near to the beloved. She rests there. She feeds on him, finding nourishment and strength from his fruit. Then she goes where he desires, because she is willing, and has the strength to go with him.

The banqueting house stands in contrast to the open field, presenting the thought of variety and abundance. Under the apple tree there were only apples. Several foods are needed for a banquet. When we come to Christ, we find life in Him—eternal life, the life of God. We may stop here, always marvelling at what God has given us at the moment of salvation, completely absorbed in the one delightful fruit of the work of Christ.

God plans that we will move from the initial enjoyment of salvation from sin's penalty, to the continuing enjoyment of being delivered from sin's power. He desires that we should expand our vision from a salvation that makes us ready for heaven, to see ourselves as channels to carry God's good news to others on earth.

The person who has life in Christ has only begun with God. Jesus said, "I am come that they might have life, and that they might have it more abundantly" (John 10:10). The trusting heart can receive life from the Son of God, risen and in heaven, but the abundant life comes from the Christ who dwells within. He pours His life, endless and vibrant with glory, through these frail bodies of ours.

"Much more!" says Paul—but what can be "much more" than being reconciled to God. "For if, when we were enemies, we were reconciled to God by the death of his Son, much more, being reconciled, we shall be saved by his life" (Romans 5:10). God sees being saved by the life of Christ as being "much more" than being saved by His death. As Christ lives the abundant life through a man, the world becomes aware that the resurrected Christ is alive and in control of the action. In God's reckoning, our reconciliation to Him is much, but His life being seen in us is much more.

The banqueting house of the abundant life is open to every Christian, but it requires surrender to find it. "He brought me," says the Shulamite. She did not find her way alone. When the shepherd was the centre of her life, he brought her to it. While she speaks about it, she is missing it, and knows what she is missing. Having lost her closeness to the shepherd, she has also lost the abundance that leaves her confused and empty. She still keeps on reaching for substitutes.

"Stay me with flagons, comfort me with apples: for I am sick of love. His left hand

*is under my head, and his right hand doth
embrace me"* (Song of Solomon 2:5–6).

Flagons and apples are likely raisins and cit-
rons respectively. Both will satisfy the appetite
and build health for the body, but they are poor
substitutes for the shepherd beloved. To understand these verses, we must remember that the
bride is in such an unusual position that she is in
danger of being separated from her shepherd forever. She has been thinking of the good days when
they were together, but now she realizes that it
might all be past, and feels the hollow emptiness of
life without him. She feels sick and depressed.

It is love that makes her feel depressed. This
gives a clue to the meaning of her next words.
They are written in the present tense, but many
authorities concur that this passage should be, "Let
his left hand be under my head and his right hand
embrace me."

Temporarily aware of her loss, the Shulamite
is willing to submit to the absent shepherd, knowing that the true experience of love that will satisfy
her heart must be shared with him alone. The word
"let" is very significant here. The Lord will never
force us to yield to Him. We must let Him take
possession of our lives. "Submit yourselves therefore to God," James taught. It is in submitting
that we begin to feel the constant touch of His
great love.

We who are Christians never need to feel
despair that the Lover is absent, and unable to
hear, as our hearts breathe submission and surrender to Him. These are the words He has been waiting to hear ever since the hour of our salvation.

*"I charge you, O ye daughters of Jerusalem,
by the roes, and by the hinds of the field,
that ye stir not up, nor awake my love, till
he please"* (Song of Solomon 2:7).

The daughters of Jerusalem could change their
geographic location, but their citizenship and iden-
tity were still linked with the city from which they
had come. They belonged there. The city and its
king had become the focal point of everything that
happened in their lives.

The Shulamite was a real puzzle to these
women. They could not understand her fidelity to
the shepherd, when the alternative was the wealthy
Solomon. It seems evident that they pressured her
to give up and conform to Solomon's wishes. Several times during the Song, the Shulamite pleads
with them, almost orders them, not to do this.

These city girls were not very interested in the
deer on the Bether mountains. The Shulamite
watched them. Free to choose where they would
run and what they would do, they stood as a symbol to her of her right to choose whom she would
love and serve, and how she would spend her life.
We see her at one of the windows, pointing to the
roes and the hinds as they climb the surrounding
hills. She demands that the other girls leave her
alone to choose to love Solomon, or to reject him.

The words, "until he please" could be translated "until it please" as in the English Revised
Version. It is our inward love that ultimately
chooses where and how we will spend our lives. The
Shulamite had been besieged by Solomon, his
things, and his people. He was presented as the
only reasonable choice. The shepherd just did not

count. She almost seems to agree with them on several occasions, and she asks to be left alone to make her decision, but she is never left alone to do this.

We must respond to the Lord Jesus while a barrage of tempters and temptations try to draw us away from Him. His one voice with His unique appeal is the great love offer of our lives. We cannot wait until the clamour quietens. It is now that we need to hear Him. We will never have the luxury of unchallenged commitment to our Beloved.

Chapter 6

HESITATION IS HURTFUL

The Shulamite was growing accustomed to her new life in the valley residence. So much of it was like her home in Shunem—the vines, the flowers, the deer running across the nearby slopes—but with the added benefit that the struggle of living was gone. She now loved the fox puppies and the luxurious appointments of her new home. She missed the shepherd less and less. In fact, she often got so involved with the activities of each new day that he was out of her mind completely for hours at a time.

Suddenly, the shepherd's call comes cascading into the new life she is making. She knows it is he, somewhere out on the mountains, giving the call she had so often heard as he gathered his sheep to return them to the fold. No one else had a call like that. She recognizes the voice immediately. Every fibre in her body tightens with excitement. Holding perfectly still, she listens. "The voice of my beloved!" she says within her heart.

Her pulse had often quickened its beat as the shepherd called from the distance while approaching her home in Shunem. She had listened for him then. Now she heard the voice when she was not listening.

This is how it is with our Shepherd. He speaks to us in many ways so that we will know His voice, the sound becoming precious to us, although heard only by our spiritual ears. Then when we wander from Him, we will hear His call to return, even though we will not be listening for it.

The Lord spoke one day to those who did not believe on Him, pointing out to them that the reason His words caused no response in their hearts was that they were not His followers. In contrast, He pointed out that those who really did belong to Him had a response to His voice: "My sheep hear my voice, and I know them, and they follow me" (John 10:27).

In the quietness of the valley residence, the Shulamite hears the shepherd call of her beloved. The sound means nothing to the others residing there. He has found her where she is, and is coming to see her. She can hardly believe it!

Running to the window, she scans the encircling mountains for a glimpse of him. There he is!

"Behold, he cometh leaping upon the mountains, skipping upon the hills. My beloved is like a roe or a young hart . . ."
(Song of Solomon 2:8-9).

Watching him move quickly across the rugged terrain, leaping from rock to rock, dropping into a crevasse only to appear moments later on the nearer rim, she becomes very excited, marvelling at his strength and masculine vigour. What she does not realize is that she has really been a prisoner, and that her beloved has loved her enough to scale the prison walls.

He was leaping on the mountains, running across them as if they were not obstacles at all. These surrounding hills and crags had made it impossible for the Shulamite to leave the residence if she had wanted to, or to try to return home by herself. What was impossible for her was easily accomplished by the shepherd.

This is how the Lord works in our lives. He does what we cannot do. Our problems are just stepping stones to Him. He often draws near to us on the very mountains that have become our prison.

The Psalmist looked back over a great deliverance in his life, and commented, "Before I was afflicted I went astray . . ." (Psalm 119:67), and, "It is good for me that I have been afflicted; that I might learn thy statutes" (Psalm 119:71). The affliction that could have crushed and destroyed him, was used by the Lord as a means of approach, so that his path of life and behaviour could be shared by the God who loved him.

With disdain for the winding road, the shepherd moves directly across the range of hills towards her. He moves just like a roe, or a young hart.

The roe mentioned by the Shulamite is usually called a gazelle. It is a member of the antelope family. Though only two feet high at the shoulders, the roe is a marvel of lightness and grace as it moves across the rough, rocky hillsides at great speed. The Hebrew word for roe has the thought of beauty built right into it.

The hart is a stag or male deer which grows considerably larger than the gazelle, sometimes weighing as much as three hundred pounds. As the hart climbs the mountainside, its powerful muscles portray strength in action. This appears to have so impressed the ancient people, that the name of the animal is derived from the Hebrew word for strength.

It was the strength and beauty of the beloved that stirred the girl, but it was his strength and his beauty seen from a distance. She enjoyed watching him in action, knowing that the action was evidence of his great love for her.

The Lord Jesus is omnipotent. There is nothing that He wants to do that is beyond the reach of His power. Omnipotence simply means that He has unlimited power. Jesus told His disciples, "All power is given unto me in heaven and in earth" (Matthew 28:18). Later on, the Holy Spirit explained that every hour of every day the Son of God is "upholding all things by the word of his power" (Hebrews 1:3). This power is seen in His death at Calvary for our sins. He did there what no other person could have done. Because of that historic accomplishment, He is able now "to save them to the uttermost that come unto God by him" (Hebrews 7:25). This great power of His is now made available to us.

We do not talk so freely about the beauty of the Lord as we do of His power, partly because in our culture beauty is associated with the outward appearance of a person, and the male is called handsome rather than beautiful. The beauty of the Lord Jesus is deeper than appearance. It takes in His attitudes, His words, His reactions, His warmth, and most of all, His capacity to love, and keep on loving. The total personality of the Beloved is attractive to the person who knows Him well. He is a wonderful man, commanding respect, while He stirs our emotions.

The Shulamite was excited by the beauty and the strength of the shepherd that had appealed to her so much during their courtship. However, as he drew nearer, the very qualities that had been precious at a distance, became a threat to the life she was living. The shepherd had in mind to share his strength with her, so that she might forever leave the bondage she thought was freedom. He desired to share himself with her.

Our Shepherd desires to have us enjoy His strength day by day. It is not enough for Him to be our Saviour, having us enjoy the distant work of His power at Calvary, while we anticipate another future work of power at His return. He desires to share His strength with us every day of our lives.

Paul wanted to be rid of a weakness that seemed to be hindering him as a Christian. Three times he asked God to take it away. God refused, giving as His reason: "My strength is made perfect in weakness" (2 Corinthians 12:9). Paul gradually realized that he had to feel weak, so that he would continually lean on the Lord. He learned the value of having a problem to cope with, "that the power of Christ may rest upon me" (2 Corinthians

12:9). The Lord wants us to face the challenges of life in His strength alone.

The Beloved also wants to place His beauty upon us. The world has its own images of success, confidence, independence, intellectualism, and many other facets of human behaviour. The Lord is willing to build within us His likeness, which is different from all of these, combining within a man or woman the qualities that make our Lord Jesus Christ unique as a personality. Humility will replace pride. Total dependence will replace self-confident independence. Instead of rebellious self-will, we will embrace the will of God. We will be willing to let the sinful life go, "that the life also of Jesus might be made manifest in our mortal flesh" (2 Corinthians 4:11).

The shepherd comes near to the Shulamite. She says:

> *"Behold, he standeth behind our wall, he looketh forth at the windows, showing himself through the lattice"* (Song of Solomon 2:9.

It seems to be a strange paradox that the girl found joy and excitement watching her beloved moving about in the distance, yet now that he is so close that there is just a wall between them, she hides from him instead of running into his arms.

We may live out this same paradox every day. The distant Lord who saves us from coming judgment we love, but the Lord who can save us every day from our own selves frightens us.

The wall referred to is the wall of the house itself, and not the wall surrounding the house. The

windows were simply openings in the wall with a
lattice-like wooden screen placed in the openings.

Whose wall was it? The Shulamite calls it,
"our wall," but the shepherd certainly has no part
in it. It is Solomon's wall, and the Shulamite's, as
she chooses to identify with Solomon.

Solomon had brought that separating wall into
her life, but the Shulamite, who could have elimi-
nated the barrier by taking a few simple steps,
stays behind it. The shephard comes as close as
possible, makes his presence known, then looks to
see if he may speak face to face with her. He has
come as far as he may.

The wall represents many things brought into
the lives of Christians by Satan to keep them from
close contact with their Beloved. Behind all of
these lies the reminder given by James: "To him
that knoweth to do good, and doeth it not, to him
it is sin" (James 4:17). The people of whom
James spoke were just doing the everyday things
of life; taking up residence in a city, buying, selling, and making a profit. Their sin lay in the fact
that they did not consider the will of God in what
they did. They did not do what He wanted. This
negligence on their part was recognized by James
as sin. The message he has to share is the same as
the ancient message of Isaiah, which reaches right
into our generation: "Your iniquities have separated between you and your God, and your sins
have hid his face from you" (Isaiah 59:2). Whatever stands between us and our Lord is sin. We
must step away from it.

The Shulamite knew that to step around the
wall would likely mean dying to the whole world
offered to her by Solomon: that new, exciting, mys-

terious world that she was just getting to know. Yet to remain behind it for long would result in total loss of contact with the shepherd. They would become dead to each other.

Our Beloved requires us to take a good look at our own lives from this point of view. Sin will try to come between us and the Lord. It will be a wall of separation, completely destroying our fellowship. The Lord has done everything He can do to eliminate sin from our lives. Peter says: "Who his own self bare our sins in his own body on the tree, that we, being dead to sins, should live unto righteousness: by whose stripes ye were healed" (1 Peter 2:24-25). The Saviour died so that we would become dead to sins.

Paul uses this same theme to show that we should see sin for what it is, and make a reckoning that we will be dead to sin, refusing to respond to its appeal. "How shall we, that are dead to sin, live any longer therein? . . . Reckon ye also yourselves to be dead indeed unto sin, but alive unto God through Jesus Christ our Lord" (Romans 6:2, 11). On the basis of this reckoning, the Lord will give all of His resources to bring it about. We will be alive to Him, and He to us.

The Shulamite decided against stepping around the wall. Her shepherd continued to appeal to her, phrasing it in words that she could understand.

> *"My beloved spake, and said unto me,*
> *Rise up, my love, my fair one, and come*
> *away. For, lo, the winter is past, the rain*
> *is over and gone; The flowers appear on*
> *the earth; the time of the singing of birds*

is come, and the voice of the turtle is
heard in our land; The fig tree putteth
forth her green figs, and the vines with
the tender grape give a good smell. Arise,
my love, my fair one, and come away"
            (Song of Solomon 2:10-13).

The shepherd calls for her. His invitation puts
into words the feelings of his heart. He tells her
why she should come. He is speaking to the girl he
expects to marry, a girl with whom he has spent
many hours. Between them there would exist that
private communication that says more than the
words. They have a conversation within a conversation which would be missed by anyone who over-
heard.

His mention of winter indicates that they
have been separated for some months. The cold
had kept him away; not because it was too cold for
him, but because he knew that she could not
weather the cold trip back home. He is explaining
why he waited so long to come. His care for her
shows in the mention of it. The coldness of the
winter had been amplified because he had missed
her company, and the pleasure of her nearness.
This, like the winter, should now be in the past.

The rains were no great problem to the shepherd. He was accustomed to the slimy mud, the
swollen creeks, and the wet night chill. For her, the
dangers brought by the torrential rains would have
been too much. Discouragement and exhaustion
would have overcome her. Not only were the rains
over; they were also gone. Natural drainage had
taken place. The creeks had returned to normal,

and the paths and roads had hard surfaces again. Her foot would not slip.

Throughout the Song various flowers are mentioned. These had great appeal to the Shulamite, and had no doubt given them much mutual joy. The flowers that "appear" stand in contrast to the cultured flowers in the gardens of Solomon. He refers to the lily and the rose that grew wild in the valleys and on the plain. Significantly, she was the flower that had not appeared.

It was the time of singing. The phrase "of birds" is in italics indicating that it was not in the original manuscripts. The singing that she normally was part of, required her. The migrating turtledove had returned, and was making its music, but she had not returned. It was time for her to return. She should stay away no longer.

The fruit of the fig tree begins to grow before the winter, remains green and small through the winter, and fills with juice when it turns red in the spring. The Shulamite would quickly recognize a reference to the fruit of their love, held dormant for a time, but now ready to sweeten and grow.

She had often walked through her own vineyard, enjoying the fragrance of the tender growing grapes in the spring time. The work of pruning and tying suddenly proved worth the effort as the savour of life flowed through the vines. There is a suggestion in his words that he is speaking of her vineyard, that it has known his care in her absence, and that she should come with him now to enjoy it while the fragrance she loved was still in the air.

The shepherd has beautifully tied together all of the things that would reach her heart; the winter, the rains, the flowers, the singing, the turtle-dove, the fig tree, and the vines. With every reference he was saying, "I love you, why don't you come with me?" She still hesitates, and remains on the wrong side of the wall.

Our Shepherd reaches for us in the cold hardness of our rejection of His will, when so often our feet are slipping and we do not even realize it. While we are resisting His call, we miss the beauty He wants to build into our lives, and the song He is able to give us. If we do respond to Him, He will bring the fruit from our hearts, so long chilled and dormant, so that the fragrance of fruitful spiritual life will again surround us.

The silence remains unbroken. No movement is made by the Shulamite to join him. The shepherd calls again. This time his appeal is personal and direct.

"Oh my dove, that art in the clefts of the rock, in the secret places of the stairs, let me see thy countenance, let me hear thy voice; for sweet is thy voice and thy countenance is comely" (Song of Solomon 2:14).

Both possession and responsibility show in the expression, "My dove." As the dove was defence-less and needed to be protected, so the Shulamite needed protection and care. Although the girl did not seem to realize this, it was very clear to the shepherd. He had accepted this responsibility willingly at the time of their betrothal, but could only carry it out with her continuing consent.

The phrase "clefts of the rock," has been romanticized to the point that it is almost possible to think of it having a negative connotation. However, in the context of the Song there can be no doubt that the Shulamite was hiding from the shepherd. She did not want to give up the rich life that she had found, or at least she was hesitating to give it up. It is very likely that the house built by Solomon in Bethabara was constructed of stone covered with cedar. This is not stated, but we do have evidence that Solomon preferred to have great rocks adding mass to his dwellings. The Scripture tells us of the temple, of Solomon's own house, and of the house he built for Pharaoh's daughter, one of his wives: "All these were of costly stones, according to the measures of hewed stones, sawed with saws, within and without, even from the foundation unto the coping, and so on the outside toward the great court. And the foundation was of costly stones, even great stones, stones of ten cubits, and stones of eight cubits. And above were costly stones, after the measures of hewed stones, and cedars . . ." (1 Kings 7:9-11).

The beloved would be looking into the interior of a house of heavy construction from the window. Unable to see the maiden, he would know that she was either in a rift in the rocks, or in one of the stair wells, where she was out of his line of vision.

Why would he still try to reach her in spite of such total rejection? Two answers are immediately evident. Firstly, he loved her with a truly great love. Secondly, he knew that she still loved him, but was confused by the immensity of the temptation.

His love shows in the words he uses. He wants so much to see her face again, and to hear her voice. For many months he had waited for this moment. It was almost more than he could bear to be so close, yet to neither see nor hear her. To him, hers was the most beautiful face of all, the template of it being daily imprinted upon his heart.

No voice stirred his emotions like hers. All he desired of life was that he might share it with her. She had promised that this longing of his would be satisfied during the months of courtship as they moved towards the time when their promises would become vows. Now, when she had stepped aside from every commitment she had ever made to him, he awaits her answer. It is a most unusual answer.

"Take us the foxes, the little foxes, that spoil the vines: for our vines have tender grapes. My beloved is mine, and I am his: he feedeth among the lilies. Until the day break, and the shadows flee away, turn, my beloved, and be thou like a roe or a young hart upon the mountains of Bether" (Song of Solomon 2:15-17).

The words of the shepherd have broken down some of the barriers. The Shulamite loves him, but he still does not have all of her affection.

During the weeks of winter, she had grown attached to the little fox puppies. She could not leave them behind. They must come with her to Shunem. Almost before she finished, she remembered that while little foxes are fun in a garden, they have no place in a vineyard. Their very nature made them destructive to the vines. Foxes eat the tender grapes, dig holes and passages around the vine roots, and gnaw the stems and young shoots.

It was a very special vineyard that would be endangered by the little foxes. She speaks of "our vines," as having tender grapes. It is the vineyard back in Shunem. It becomes clear that she must make the choice between the little foxes and the shepherd. The shepherd is not interested in anything that belongs to Solomon. While Solomon is not now in the picture, his toys have indeed become a snare.

The Christian may not be attracted to Satan, however cunningly he may disguise himself, but the playthings he offers have trapped many hearts.

The Shulamite now makes a reckoning of her own; not the reckoning we thought of earlier, where she would go with the shepherd, having reckoned herself dead to Solomon and his proposals. Rather, she reckons on the total reliability of the shepherd and the constancy of his love.

"My beloved is mine," she says, sounding like the Christian who claims security while he walks away from the Lord. She is right! All of her coldness, rejection, and indecision have not changed his love. This she can depend on. "And I am his," she continues, meanwhile forgetting that she shows no sign that she means it.

The forthrightness of her statement is parallel to Jonah's confession of faith. He totally rejected God's will for him, and was travelling away from his Divinely appointed mission-field in a ship caught in a fearful storm. Yet when one of the sailors asked him about his occupation and his nationality, anticipating disaster at sea, Jonah replied, "I am an Hebrew; and I fear the Lord" (Jonah 1:9). He claimed to fear the God he was rejecting.

Taking the shepherd completely for granted, the Shulamite says, "He feedeth among the lilies." In other words she is saying, "I know where to find him if I want him." One point in her reckoning was away out of line, but she could not see this. The lily-covered valleys where her beloved fed his flock were many miles away, far across the Bether mountains, and through dangerous country she could never navigate on her own. She asked him to give her until morning to make her final decision.

The most significant word in the final verse of the chapter is "turn." The shepherd had come the many miles from home to see and talk with her, and if possible to take her home. He now realizes that there is nothing to keep her from him but her own desire to stay with Solomon. While she is undecided, she asks him to be like he was earlier in the day, distant, but beautiful and strong in the distance, like the roe and the young hart.

The name of the mountain range has an unusual message for us. Bether means "a part or a piece," according to G. V. Wigram. The great truth contained in the chapter is thus summed up in one word. While the Lord has given all for us, we are often willing to give Him only a piece of our lives, reserving the rest for ourselves. The result of giving a part of your life to the Lord is that it really means giving Him the outside place. The fellowship and love He longs for is denied Him, while He remains faithful, outside, but still the waiting Lover.

Chapter 7

KNOW WHAT MATTERS

Just before parting, the bride assured the shepherd that she would have her mind made up by morning. That was all the time she asked for. She had a momentous decision to make. We would expect her to consider the possibilities from all angles, lying awake into the hours of night, finally sleeping when satisfied that she had made the right decision.

Hesitation like this usually means that the decision has already been arrived at, and that what makes the person hesitate is the unpleasantness of breaking the news.

The shepherd bunked down in the cold outdoors, somewhere in the foothills of the Bether mountains. Inside the residence, the Shulamite popped into her soft spacious bed, pulled the fleecy covers up, and was soon asleep. It seems as if she had satisfied herself that she would be most foolish to leave this luxury, comfort, and wealth, to return to the tent life of the shepherd who waited for her. The morning would settle it once for all.

During the night her sleep was disturbed. She tells of the experience:

> *"By night on my bed I sought him whom my soul loveth: I sought him, but I found him not* (Song of Solomon 3:1).

How do you look for a person on a bed? The farthest he could move away would still be within easy reach. Only one explanation of these unusual words is possible. The Shulamite had a nightmare. Somehow, with her reasoning mind at rest, her soul made the discovery that the real love of her life was the shepherd. As a result, she repeats four times in the few verses that the shepherd was the one, "whom my soul loveth." While he was waiting, while he was near, and while she was sure that he would return, her heart had been indifferent. She felt secure because of his love. Now she was aware that this would be the final dismissal. Reaching for him time and again in her distorted dream, she saw him always beyond her reach as she tossed around in the bed, changed now from a haven of luxurious rest to a nest of terrors.

Intruding into her understanding came the repeated truth of tomorrow, and all of the tomorrows if she continued her rejection—"I found him not." It was too much for her.

All that Solomon had, everything he could give, had now faded in the darkness. The one light in her life began to show again. Without the shepherd, she could not live anything but a shallow half-life. Everything was hollow, empty, and bleak without him. Breaking from the captivity of sleep, she knew what she must do.

> *"I will rise now, and go about the city
> in the streets, and in the broad ways I
> will seek him whom my soul loveth ..."*
>   (Song of Solomon 3:2).

Stirred by her love response to the shepherd, she would allow nothing to keep her from him. The most important thing in her mind was to find him and to go with him. The emphasis in her words is present tense—"now." It immediately became intolerable to her to leave the shepherd out on the hills, while she enjoyed the soft living offered her by Solomon.

In Psalm 116, the Psalmist declares his love for the Lord in the first verse. In the verses that follow, he resolves several times to respond to the Lord he loves. "I will walk before the Lord ..." (v. 9). "I will take the cup of salvation, and (I will) call upon the name of the Lord" (v. 13). "I will pay my vows unto the Lord now in the presence of all his people" (vs. 14, 18). "O Lord, truly I am thy servant ..." (v. 16). The soul that has been stirred to love the Lord will desire continual relationship with Him. Time spent out of His fellowship, or contrary to His will, then becomes a nuisance to be avoided, an intolerable loss and waste.

Though it is still night, she says, "I will rise now ... I will seek him ..." She is no longer hesitant about following the right decision, so there was no need for her to continue to be separated

from the shepherd. This is no longer the dream. It
is her action in real life. She leaves Solomon's
things behind, and searches in the dark night, up
and down the streets and roads. The results of the
search for some time were identical with her nightmare.

> *"I sought him, but I found him not"*
> (Song of Solomon 3:2).

In her dream she had seen the tragedy of living without the man she loved. Now in her most
fervent attempts to find him, she draws a blank.
While it was certainly the right thing for her to
rise and seek, this alone was not enough. To find
him, she had to know where he was, and how to get
to that place from where she was.

Our Shepherd has made it clear to us that He
is "holy, harmless, undefiled, separate from sinners
..." (Hebrews 7:26). We will always find Him in
the place of holiness, never in the place of sin or
defilement. Therefore if we walk in sin, we cannot
walk with Him. John understood this well, and included the truth in his first epistle: "If we say that
we have fellowship with him, and walk in darkness,
we lie, and do not the truth" (1 John 1:6). John
knew that there was no darkness at all in the Lord,
and that those who are defiled with sin cannot be
His partners.

The good news from John is that he found the
way back for those who are away from the Lord. It
is the way of confession. While it is right to rise up
from where we are in the darkness to seek the
Lord, we will only find Him if we are willing to
confess and leave the sins that we know are in our

lives. The promise of forgiveness is directly linked with our willingness to confess our sins to God. John goes on to teach that, "If we confess our sins, he is faithful and just to forgive our sins, and to cleanse us from all unrighteousness" (1 John 1:9).

In His wonderful justice, the Lord listens as we confess our sins partially, knowing that we can never see all our sins as He does. When we have confessed all the sins we know about, He wipes the record clean. We are cleansed persons. All of our unrighteousness is gone because our loving Lord understood the repentant attitude of our surrendered hearts.

It was not just the shepherd that the Shulamite missed. She failed to see the watchmen of the city as well, but they found her.

> *"The watchmen that go about the city found me: to whom I said, Saw ye him whom my soul loveth?"*
> (Song of Solomon 3:3).

The watchmen watched over the people during the night. Aware of the possible dangers, they kept their eyes open while other eyes were closed. They listened, while the sleepers lost their awareness.

Paul speaks of men like these in the New Testament church: "Obey them that have the rule over you, and submit yourselves: for they watch for your souls, as they that must give account, that they may do it with joy, and not with grief: for that is unprofitable for you" (Hebrews 13:17). These watchmen of the church, often called elders or overseers, are not novices. They have maturity to recognize danger, and to give needed instruction to the person in danger of spiritual night.

The Shulamite had failed to see these men. This is normal for those who have lost contact with the Shepherd. For them, the spiritual counsellor seems to be of little consequence. However, God has His own set of values. He counts these men of special worth, and has a unique reward for those who are faithful to Him in this particular service. He used Peter to give them instruction: "Feed the flock of God which is among you, taking the oversight thereof, not by constraint, but willingly; not for filthy lucre, but of a ready mind; neither as being lords over God's heritage, but being ensamples to the flock. And when the chief Shepherd shall appear, ye shall receive a crown of glory that fadeth not away" (1 Peter 5:2-4).

No record is given of the interchange that took place between the watchmen and the Shulamite. Their counsel is kept secret. Whether their advice was helpful or not, we do know the maiden's story:

> *"It was but a little that I passed from them, but I found him whom my soul loveth: I held him, and would not let him go, until I had brought him into my mother's house, and into the chamber of her that conceived me"*
>
> (Song of Solomon 3:4).

The expression, "I held him," is a reflection of her inmost feelings, the responses of her soul. Through weakness she had been out of touch. She feels now that all this is past, and thinks she will never allow such alienation again.

As Paul speaks of Jesus' lordship in the New Testament, he brings out the thought of holding on to Him. "As ye have therefore received Christ Jesus the Lord, so walk ye in him: rooted and built up in him, and stablished in the faith . . ." (Colossians 2:6-7). According to Strong's Concordance, the word "received" is made up of two other words which together mean "to receive near." One of the root words means "to take . . . to get hold of . . ."

The Bible makes a distinction between receiving Jesus as Saviour, and receiving Him as Lord. These two different words are used to point out the difference. In John 1:12, where we are told that "as many as received him, to them gave he power to become the sons of God. . . ." the new birth is in view. The word just means to take hold of Jesus. The compound word is used in Colossians 2:6; "ye received Christ Jesus the Lord," meaning to take Him alongside. Walking with the Lord, living right with Him alongside, is what is taught here.

Since the word that relates to receiving the Saviour is part of the word that is used of receiving Christ the Lord, it seems evident that the Lord teaches that there is more to Christian experience than just knowing that you are saved. The added dimension is the word, "para," in the Greek which often appears in our English language meaning beside, or alongside.

We receive Jesus Christ as our Saviour when we take hold of Him by faith for the salvation of our souls. We receive Him as Lord when we take our place by His side, and begin to really walk with Him, all day, every day.

The Shulamite is a beautiful picture of this truth as she holds to the shepherd. She refuses to let him go. They walk through the night across the surrounding hills, not stopping until they reach Shunem and the family home. "I brought him. . . ," she says, but we understand who really did the bringing. All of the ability and strength of the shepherd became available to her as soon as she was willing to take her place by his side. He knew how to get her across the mountains that were impossible for her to cross alone. She allowed him to be to her what he wanted to be. Immediately she could do the impossible. She moved with his strength and wisdom. He moved, because she now willed to have him with her.

Our relation to the Lord is parallel to this. He desires to bring into our lives all that He is and all that He has. He will not force Himself upon us. If our will responds to His appeal, we have the option of walking in His strength, seeing the impossible repeatedly become possible. We bring Him with us by an act of will. Then He brings us with Him.

The shepherd and the Shulamite cross the threshold and enter her family home. She brings her beloved among those who love her, but who are well acquainted with her weaknesses.

It is in the home and with our immediate families that we most easily walk alone, but it is here most of all that we need to bring the sweetness of our fellowship with the Son of God.

Jesus taught this during His ministry in the country of the Gadarenes. He had delivered a man from the control of the devil, and was giving him instruction for his future life. He said, "Go home to thy friends, and tell them how great things the

Lord hath done for thee, and hath had compassion on thee (Mark 5:19)." This was the first commission, and the first mission field, for the man who had been helped. It is the same in our case.

> *"I charge you, O ye daughters of Jerusalem, by the roes, and by the hinds of the field, that ye stir not up, nor awake my love, till he please"* (Song of Solomon 3:5).

The family is together in the home in Shunem. The shepherd enjoys their home with them. The Shulamite remembers with pleasure how she had told the daughters of Jerusalem to leave her alone, not to stir up her love response, but to allow her to choose for herself. She had wanted to be free as the roes and the hinds of the field. Her willingness to wait had brought her to this moment. Love for the shepherd flooded through her. She was so glad she had chosen him.

The peace she now had seemed to block the way for any further interference from Solomon, but life is not like that. When we feel most secure with the Shepherd, the enemy is preparing another attack. In the very next verse, we read of Solomon moving through the wilderness to the town of Shunem.

Chapter 8

IT MAY BE LUST

The people of Shunem stop to look at a great cloud of dust that rises from the road leading into town. Even before they can make out the people, they know a large crowd is moving toward them.

"Who is this?" they ask of one another.

"Who is this that cometh out of the wilderness like pillars of smoke, perfumed with myrrh and frankincense, with all powders of the merchant? Behold his bed, which is Solomon's; threescore valiant men are about it, of the valiant of Israel. They all hold swords, being expert in war: every man hath his sword upon his thigh, because of fear in the night" (Song of Solomon 3:6-8).

It was Solomon, king of the nation of Israel, coming to take the Shulamite back to Jerusalem with him. The Holy Spirit uses the word "smoke" in the passage to convey to our minds the fact that Solomon is angry. Strong points out in his Concordance that the Hebrew word used for "smoke" can refer literally or figuratively to vapor, dust, or anger, and that it comes from a root word which means to be angry.

The king's anger would never show while in Shunem. It would be carefully disguised so that his mission would be thought of as a love journey, made because of the depths of his love for the beautiful maiden. Keep in mind that Solomon is the seducer, working overtime to draw the affection of the Shulamite from her betrothed. His only real goal is to have a successful conquest. Then the maid from Shunem will be relegated to the emptiness of harem life, while the king looks for another beauty to satiate his lust.

We have the double picture of Solomon, representing the evil one, as seen by Peter and by Paul. Peter says, "Your adversary the devil, as a roaring lion, walketh about, seeking whom he may devour" (1 Peter 5:8). Paul shows the other side, ". . . no marvel; for Satan himself is transformed into an angel of light" (2 Corinthians 11:14). On the one hand, absolutely evil; on the other, appearing as the ultimate in goodness.

Solomon was always accompanied with perfumes. It seems as if the mingled fragrances were so intense that the breeze carried them across the fields to reach the villagers in advance of the king. Myrrh and frankincense are first identified, and then the conglomerate is too much. The odors of these two would be quickly recognized by Hebrew people who brought the frankincense with their meal offerings, and who used the myrrh in the holy anointing oil, so vital in the consecration of their priests.

Anxious to see their king in a good light, the people would not openly conclude that Solomon, with all the powders of the merchant, really was a merchant on business, interested only in himself and his own desires, caring nothing for the populace of Shunem.

The people do not speak to each other of his majesty as he draws near, nor of his wisdom. They are not taken up with the words of their great king. Their comment is base in its intent: "Behold his bed, which is Solomon's ..." The thing that the people of Israel saw was Solomon's bed. Noted for his many amorous activities, he had the people accepting this as normal kingly behaviour.

Of the several Hebrew words which could have been chosen for "bed," Strong says that the one used by the Holy Spirit comes from a primitive root word meaning, "to stretch or spread out; by implication, to bend away (including moral deflection)." The root word is also used in the sense of causing to yield by the harlot of the proverbs: "With her much fair speech she caused him to yield, with the flattering of her lips she forced him" (Proverbs 7:21). The Lord shows through the words He chooses, that Solomon was actively engaged in continuing seduction. The people had almost begun to think it one of his attractive traits.

It seems as if Solomon obtained his satisfaction by having a continuous line of different women yield to him. The lasting love between husband and wife was not his objective. His quest was for lust, not love.

Satan desires to have us yield to him, not that he might ever meet any need of ours, but that he might destroy what good is in us. He then will leave us spiritually bankrupt, and out of fellowship with the Lord. The Lord explained how this was about to happen to Peter: "Simon, Simon, behold, Satan hath desired to have you, that he may sift you as wheat: But I have prayed for thee, that thy faith fail not: and when thou art converted, strengthen thy brethren" (Luke 22:31-32). When wheat is sifted, the grain drops through and only the chaff remains in the sieve. In contrast, the Lord winnows His people, allowing the wind to blow away the chaff, while the good kernel remains separated from the dross. It is when Satan sifts us that our relationship with the Lord is in danger.

There is no evidence in the Song that the Shulamite ever doubted the shepherd's intentions, or his absolute faithfulness. This held her steady even when she felt very weak and vulnerable. Faith on our part toward our Beloved will keep us from ever asking why He does what He does.

Around Solomon's bed sixty valiant men marched, or rode on horseback. They must keep the king safe. This would be a worthy task if the king was moving under God's control. However, it degenerates into a farce when the king uses his valiant men to protect him while he hunts girls, literally making the soldiers guardians of the bedchamber. These men were expert in war, with swords in their hands, ready for battle. They could have been fighting the enemies of the Lord, but were rather assisting the backslidden king to conquer virtuous maidens to slake his lust. Everything good had become distorted, until only the shell and the appearance of order remained.

Solomon was anointed of the Lord for his office. He was given great wisdom to perform his role of leadership. Directed by the Lord, he had built a magnificent temple for holy worship. His greatness became too much for him. He began to spend himself in lust and vanity, describing so much of it with his own pen in the book of Ecclesiastes. Much of his life was spent away from God, and in his old age, the wisest of men had truly to be reckoned a fool.

This parallels the story of Lucifer very closely. Lucifer was so exalted, so powerful, and so radiant with glory that the prophet Isaiah could hardly believe that he had fallen so far. "How art thou fallen from heaven, O Lucifer, son of the morning! how art thou cut down to the ground . . ." (Isaiah 14:12).

Speaking of Satan's early age, the prophet Ezekiel tells of Lucifer's wisdom and beauty that were so much a part of his person. "Thus saith the Lord God; Thou sealest up the sum, full of wisdom, and perfect in beauty" (Ezekiel 28:12). Like Solomon, he had the great capacity for wisdom as a gift from God. At the time of his creation, two special characteristics seem to have been built into him. Ezekiel says: "The workmanship of thy tabrets and of thy pipes was prepared in thee in the day that thou wast created" (Ezekiel 28:13). The tabret has a link with the word tamborine in our language. Lucifer moved with music accompanying his motion. The word "pipes" refers to the setting for a precious gem which would hold it to best advantage. It refers to an ability given to Lucifer by

his Creator to reflect in a special way the glory of
God which could never belong to a creature, but
which could be reflected from one. He had so much
to begin with.

Like Solomon, Lucifer had much to do with
the holiness of God and the worship due to Him.
In this particular sphere he did a majestic service
described by the God who was there. "Thou art the
anointed cherub that covereth; and I have set thee
so: thou wast upon the holy mountain of God;
thou hast walked up and down in the midst of the
stones of fire. Thou wast perfect in thy ways from
the day that thou wast created, till iniquity was
found in thee" (Ezekiel 28:14-15).

Sin spoiled all of this. Isaiah tells us that Lucifer was close to God but desired to be considered
God's equal. "And thou saidst in thy heart, I will
ascend into heaven, I will exalt my throne above
the stars of God; and I will sit upon the mount of
congregation, in the uttermost parts of the north; I
will ascend above the heights of the clouds; I will
make myself like the Most High" (Isaiah 14:13-
14 A.S.V.). This great servant, created to do the
will of his Creator, now had a will that was contrary to the Creator's will. He had sinned, his wisdom was corrupted, his sanctuaries were defiled, his
destiny was judgment.

There was no hope for him. A careful reading
of the text tells us God's words in condemnation
refer to a total change from what he was, that
would never be reversed and corrected: "Thou
shalt be a terror, and never ... thou ... any more"
(Ezekiel 28:19).

There can be little doubt that part of the trip
to Shunem was made during the hours of darkness.

The valiant men had their swords on their thighs "because of fear in the night." We seldom associate fear with Satan, looking on him more as the cause of fear than the creature who feels the emotion.

Satan knows the Scriptures well. At the time of the Lord's temptation, he quoted from them with ease. These same Scriptures have an abundance of data about the final judgment of the serpent. Though he may feel that he will have ultimate triumph in spite of the Creator's words, there must be a gnawing fear as he moves in his own night, remembering that the Lord has never yet failed to keep His promises, whether of blessing or of judgment.

> *"King Solomon made himself a chariot of the wood of Lebanon. He made the pillars thereof of silver, the bottom thereof of gold, the covering of it of purple, the midst thereof being paved with love, for the daughters of Jerusalem"*
> (Song of Solomon 3:9-10).

Solomon's total self-absorption shows in the chariot of state he built. The palanquin was made for himself alone. He was willing to share it with many of the daughters of Jerusalem, but it was built for him. He would always decide how it would be used. In building it, he used the same lumber as in building God's house for the responsive hearts that had pure love toward their God. The silver, the purple, and the gold were also present as in the temple.

Outwardly the chariot was beautiful, but the inside of it was prepared for the satisfaction of the king's lust. The American Revised Version says the chariot was "paved with love, from the daughters of Jerusalem." No matter how attractive Satan's traps may be, the desired outcome is the corruption of the believer.

As though all of the years of corrupt living could be waved aside in a moment, we hear the ambition of the parents in Shunem in the final words of the chapter:

> *"Go forth, O ye daughters of Zion, and behold king Solomon with the crown wherewith his mother crowned him in the day of his espousals, and in the day of the gladness of his heart"* (Song of Solomon 3:11).

What a tragedy that the mothers of beautiful girls should feel the identification with the king was worth the loss of their daughters to his harem. They may have had in their minds the part his mother played in bringing Solomon to the throne, the joy Solomon had in receiving the throne which could easily have gone to his brother Adonijah, or the early part of his reign when he ruled under Divine control, with God-given wisdom. It was all so good in the memory, but the years of sin and self-pleasing had made a different man of Solomon. As they looked on the regal, self-confident, gracious king, all of this was hidden from their eyes.

Chapter 9

PURITY IS STILL
PRECIOUS

As the chariot waits to take the Shulamite back to Jerusalem, she has an unusual conversation with the shepherd. He knows that the maiden is under tremendous pressure to go with the king, but finds her to tell her what she means to him, and why she is so beautiful in his eyes.

In the pomp and display of the king's retinue, the glitter, noise and excitement make the shepherd, with his quiet words of love, seem insignificant. The Shulamite listens. His words are precious to her, but there seems to be no course possible but to go with the overpowering monarch. She had likely never seen such an exhibition of armed power, and may have felt that refusal would have determined one of the drawn swords for her.

Disregarding the total enemy strength, the

shepherd speaks in the few minutes that he is able to get alone with her:

> *"Behold, thou art fair, my love; behold, thou art fair; thou hast doves' eyes within thy locks: thy hair is as a flock of goats, that appear from mount Gilead"*
> (Song of Solomon 4:1).

Though she is doing what she thinks she must, the Shulamite feels that she has betrayed the shepherd by deciding to return with the king. She might have expected reproof from him, or even anger or condemnation. Instead, he tells her that she is beautiful. He repeats it, emphasizing it each time with the word, "Behold," as though he wants to write it on her mind to steady her in the temptations she will face.

He then mentions her eyes using words she has heard before. She loves them because they strengthened her at the king's banquet, invading her heart and mind while the king was trying to turn her to himself. Just as the dove watches for the absent mate, wailing for his return, the shepherd knew that there would be the reflected longing in her eyes while they were apart. The beloved never questions her love, even though all signs indicate that it is not the great love that he has for her. He sees love in her eyes for himself.

Her long hair reminds him of a flock of goats on the mountainside. Clustered together, the flock had beauty, movement, and yet order, especially as seen from a distance, since Shunem was on the opposite side of Jordan from Gilead. It may have been on the journey from Bethabara that this flock caught their attention.

Time and again in the Scriptures, hair is a symbol of submission. The Nazirite vow was only in force so long as the person refrained from using a razor on his body. The hair grew long because of a definite commitment to the Lord. Samson stands out as a notable example of what it meant to be a Nazirite. His submission to the Lord was seen in his long hair, but Delilah fought to dominate him, ultimately cutting his hair. The vow of the Nazirite was broken. The Lord was no longer obligated to make the man strong. If the Nazirite broke the vow, he was to shave his head completely, and at the conclusion of his vow he was to shave his head and burn the hair on God's altar. All of this signified that he was submissive to the Lord.

The apostle Paul writes of hair in the epistle to the Corinthians, linking it to the woman's relationship to the man—submission to him in the Lord. He concludes, "But if a woman have long hair, it is a glory to her: for her hair is given her for a covering" (1 Corinthians 11:15). The word "covering" could be rendered veil. As eastern women veiled themselves in the presence of men, the Lord has made a provision for women to show their submissive attitude by the wearing of longer hair than men.

Just as the shepherd saw in the hair of the Shulamite something that was beautiful and appealing to him, our Shepherd values the quality of meekness and submission to His control that is depicted by the mention of hair so often in Scripture. The quality of meekness makes the Christian beautiful in the Lord's eyes. Bible meekness is the attitude toward God that accepts what God does as good, with no resistance, and without disputing what He does. The meek person does not struggle against God, nor fight with Him. Among the Arab horse dealers, the word "meek" was used to depict the finest of horses. They were full of spirit and strength, and had great endurance. The chief quality they had was the submission of the will to the master, so that no move was made without his command. Meekness is a priceless treasure as the Lord sees it developed within our hearts.

The shepherd continues to speak to her:

> *"Thy teeth are like a flock of sheep that are even shorn, which came up from the washing; whereof every one bear twins, and none is barren among them"*
>
> (Song of Solomon 4:2).

In a culture where it was easy to be careless about tooth care, the Shulamite was exemplary. Her teeth were white, like a flock of newly washed sheep. They were perfectly shaped and paired with none missing, none out of line. The significant point is that the teeth were showing. She wore a smile because the beloved was near. Even in her confusion, her response to him showed that she had a joy in him.

Our joy is linked to the person of the Beloved. There is great joy in knowing and loving Him, and in sharing His love hour after hour. Peter spoke of this in his epistle: ". . . Jesus Christ: Whom having not seen, ye love; in whom, though now ye see him not, yet believing, ye rejoice with joy unspeakable and full of glory" (1 Peter 1:7-8). Just

as true human love stirs the hearts of the lovers
with joy, a real love for the Lord will build within
us joy when He is near. Paul knew that this joy
could never be within a man unless the Lord put it
there. He had no doubt seen some pretending a joy
they did not have, while others tried to create their
joy by emotional experiences or stimulating excitement. That is why he wrote so simply: "Now the
God of hope fill you with all joy and peace in believing, that ye may abound in hope, through the
power of the Holy Ghost" (Romans 15:13). Only
God can fill the Christian with joy. He fills those
who are near to Him.

Jesus emphasized this in His personal ministry
to His disciples. He compared Himself to a vine,
and the disciples to branches. He pointed out that
they needed to abide in Him, remaining as close
and as dependent as the branch of a vine to the
main stem. Then He showed them that it was His
love that made it possible for them to be so near to
Him, and that this nearness would be a lasting experience for them if they would continue in His
love, or continue resting or abiding in Him.

Why was this so important? He went on to explain: "These things have I spoken unto you, that
my joy might remain in you, and that your joy
might be full" (John 15:11). Their joy would be
multiplied as He bore fruit through them. They
would see the evidence of His love in the spiritual
fruit of their lives.

The principles of joy seem to be included in
the beloved's description in some detail which we
could easily miss on casual reading. The flock tells
of a relationship with the shepherd and fellowship
with those who are following him. Shearing indi-

cates the removal of the superfluous weight or cutting off of that which is dead. Washing focuses our attention on the need for confession and cleansing so that our joy will continue. The mention of "twins" connotes fruitfulness, emphasized by the fact that none were barren. The link between fruit and joy is mentioned by Paul to the Thessalonians: "For what is our hope, or joy, or crown of rejoicing? Are not even ye in the presence of our Lord Jesus Christ at his coming? For ye are our glory and joy" (1 Thessalonians 2:19-20).

The Holy Spirit thus hides many of the truths that relate to the Christian's joy in a simple description from the lips of a man who loves a country maid, watching her smile at him in a time of her deep distress.

The shepherd goes on to say,

"Thy lips are like a thread of scarlet, and thy speech is comely: thy temples are like a piece of a pomegranate within thy locks" (Song of Solomon 4:3).

To him, her lips were beautiful both in appearance and appeal. Red lips indicate vibrant health. The shepherd was describing the girl he loved, not artificially applied coloring. No hidden anemia drained her colour telling of inward problems. She was radiantly healthy.

God begins to build His goodness into our souls as soon as we are saved. As Christ is formed in us the goodness which characterizes Him becomes part of our persons. This is why the Psalmist could say, "He satisfieth the longing soul and filleth the hungry soul with goodness" (Psalm 107:9).

Only the Lord can put goodness within the soul of a man. This is why Paul wrote to the wealthy Philemon who had helped so many people, "every good thing which is in you in Christ Jesus" (Philemon :6). The good that was in Philemon had come into his life in the form of Jesus Christ. Paul affirms that it is essential to recognize and admit that the good in our lives is simply Christ. It is this that enables us to effectually communicate our faith.

Just as the good health of the Shulamite showed in her lips, the goodness of the soul pours through the lips of the Christian. Paul's message to the Galatians ties the two together. "Brethren, if a man be overtaken in a fault, ye which are spiritual restore such an one in the spirit of meekness; considering thyself, lest thou be tempted" (Galatians 6:1). The Greek word for "restore" in this verse is the same word used in reference to the disciples, "mending their nets" (Mark 1:19). To restore is to mend so that no weakness remains. This can only be done by the spiritual person who has the Lord's goodness within him to pour out in the aid of another. The beloved spoke of the maiden's lips as a thread of scarlet, the word "thread" coming from a root word meaning "to sew."

The Lord finds great pleasure in us as we pour out of the goodness that He has put into our soul so that another damaged life can be mended and made whole again. The Lord puts the goodness— the abundant life—within, so that He can minister through us, using us to bless and help in other's lives.

How easy it is to forget this principle and to use our lips to condemn the sinning saint. "Thy speech is comely," says the shepherd, using a word meaning suitable or beautiful. Her words were suited to her person, and thus were beautiful in his estimation. She spoke no ugly words. Her words reflected what she was within herself.

Now if this seems to be a bit theoretical, listen to the teaching of the Lord through James. "For every kind of beasts, and of birds, and of serpents, and of things in the sea, is tamed, and hath been tamed of mankind: But the tongue can no man tame; it is an unruly evil, full of deadly poison" (James 3:7-8). The Christian cannot tame his tongue. God must do that; but God's method is to change the man on the inside. Then everything falls into place. The man controlled by God has control over his speech because this also has been given to the Lord. Our Shepherd finds great joy in controlled, God-honouring use of words.

The shepherd next speaks of the Shulamite's temples, claiming that they look like a piece of pomegranate. The thin skin of the pomegranate tells of what lies beneath it, the tasty seeds contained in separate pulp sacks, sweet and tangy to the taste. While we normally think of the temple as a small section of the forehead above and behind the outside corner of each eye, it really refers to quite a large area. Strong interprets the word as meaning simply the sides of the head.

The temple lies over a portion of the conscious brain. It is the part of the brain that does not work automatically, but is under the control of a person's will. In this area of the brain, a person puts things together from memory, makes judgments, and plans his behaviour. It is the portion of the brain that becomes disoriented, and confused when the terrors become too great, the difficulties too tremendous, and the trembling human searches for answers that are not there.

The Lord spoke of times that would tax the believer if he tried to face them as thinking man alone. He explained this to His disciples. "Ye shall hear of wars and rumours of wars ... For nation shall rise against nation, and kingdom against kingdom: and there shall be famines, and pestilences, and earthquakes, in divers places. All these are the beginning of sorrows. Then shall they deliver you up to be afflicted, and shall kill you: and ye shall be hated of all nations for my name's sake. And then shall many be offended, and shall betray one another, and shall hate one another" (Matthew 24:6-10).

What does a man do in times like these? We know from history that he often becomes hard and cruel. He may even sacrifice every principle he has for mere existence, or he may crumble mentally and escape from it all by losing his sense of reality. To the disciples the Lord's instructions were clear: "See that ye be not troubled: for all these things must come to pass" (Matthew 24:6). The word He used for "troubled" means to wail, to clamor, or to be frightened. He expected them to have peace in their minds when everything around them was calling for the reaction of fear and hopelessness.

The Lord did not comfort them about the future terrors by saying that everything would be alright. Rather, He assured them that some would die while others would be hurt and hated. He was asking of them more than mere man could give, but then, He planned to make them more than mere men. While still with them He spoke of the peace He was giving them, peace that He had possessed in His lifetime: "Peace I leave with you, my peace I give unto you: not as the world giveth, give I unto you. Let not your heart be troubled, neither let it be afraid" (John 14:27).

Later in His teaching, He emphasized that the peace they would have would be directly related to Him as a person: "These things I have spoken unto you, that in me ye might have peace" (John 16:33). It was in Him their peace would originate, just as in His own loneliness and rejection He had peace because of His continuing fellowship with the Father.

The disciples learned their lesson well. Long after, we hear Peter teaching in Caesarea that peace is found in Jesus Christ and that it is related to a right understanding of who He is—"The word which God sent unto the children of Israel, preaching peace by Jesus Christ: (he is Lord of all)" (Acts 10:36). When we know the true greatness of the Lord; that He has all power as well as great love, we are able to move in peace through the troubles that break over us. It is faith, our simple trust directed toward the Son of God, that brings this peace into our lives.

Paul implies faith as he speaks of the Christian praying in Philippians 4:6. The very next verse promises: "And the peace of God, which passeth all understanding, shall keep your hearts and minds through Christ Jesus." If we know the Lord well enough to trust Him implicitly, we will be able to claim the peace which He has given, and to experience it without pretense, when everything around us seems to be in danger of shaking loose.

The Lord desires to see in us that simple trust that believes the "Lord of all" knows how to handle our most complicated problems.

The shepherd mentions that both the eyes of the maiden, and her temples, are "within thy locks." This links both the eyes and the temples with the teaching of the hair. The long locks of hair hung down each side of the Shulamite's face. In other words, the love in the eyes, and the peace in the mind, relate directly to our recognition of Jesus as Lord, and our willing submission to His lordship. This frames our love for Him and our peace in Him, putting it in proper perspective. As we fix our spiritual eyes on Him, we can trust His love to show us the way that we must go, while we lean on His power to carry us through.

Two further areas of delight are spoken of by the shepherd:

> *"Thy neck is like the tower of David builded for an armoury, whereon there hang a thousand bucklers, all shields of mighty men. Thy two breasts are like two young roes that are twins, which feed among the lilies"* (Song of Solomon 4:4-5).

The tower of David was not simply built as a lookout for protection of a city, flock, or vineyard, as so many others were. It was built to be an armoury, where men would keep their fighting equipment in order between battles. The significance of the reference is that the bucklers and the shields were all in place. No battle was being fought. At the time of these events, Israel was a nation at peace, using its strength in commerce rather than wars.

Something in the gentleness of the maiden's neck stirred the shepherd. It was not the craning, mobile, aggressive neck, straining to fight, conquer, and accomplish. Nor was it the stiff, unbending neck that the Lord spoke about to characterize His people when they were rebellious.

The Lord works to produce a gentleness in us who love Him. He will name us His servants only if that quality has been developed. Paul teaches that, "The servant of the Lord must not strive; but be gentle unto all men, apt to teach, patient" (2 Timothy 2:24). Gentleness in human behaviour, particularly when serving the Lord, is a basic recognition that man does not need to fight the battles of the Lord. He has but to stand with the Lord while the Lord grants the victory.

We can readily understand the shepherd finding joy in the beauty and form of the Shulamite as he speaks of her breasts being like twin roes feeding among the lilies on the pasture. Let us also remember that the human breast is for nurturing the infant who does not know what he needs, but is able to recognize it when he is fed. Psychologists now know that normal emotional development in a child is aided by the softness and warmth of the breasts of his mother.

Several times in the Song the shepherd is the one who nurtures the maiden, helping her in her fear and uncertainty until she is ready to go on again. In this he represents the Lord in a special way. One of God's Old Testament names is "El Shaddai" which means "the breasted one." Jehovah is Shaddai because He nourishes those who trust in Him and gives them strength.

However, while El Shaddai is willing to pour out of His abundance, His long-suffering is seen in His willingness to wait to make His abundance available to His people. Very often they rejected the nurture of the Lord. Moses had evidently heard God's instruction on this very level: "Carry them in thy bosom, as a nursing father beareth the sucking child" (Numbers 11:12). He had suffered long with them through countless problems and quoted these words to the Lord when he felt he had nothing left to give.

Paul also speaks to the followers of the Lord in a different age and culture bringing together the spirit of his own ministry as being like a nurse with her own children, while caring as a father for them. "But we were gentle among you, even as a nurse cherisheth her children" (1 Thessalonians 2:7). "Ye know how we exhorted and comforted and charged every one of you, as a father doth his children" (1 Thessalonians 2:11). The nurse is different with her own children than with any others who come under her care. The father may show interest in many children, but his own children are special to him, receiving all that he might give to another child, but so much more because of the love of father relationship.

As the shepherd spoke with admiration of the breasts of the Shulamite, seeing in them two of God's creatures on the pasture lands of the valleys, he may have thought of her ability to nurture and care for the children they hoped to have together.

He also recognized in her an ability to care with forbearance where necessary, since this is involved in feeding and tending.

He saw in her the things that pleased him. He paralleled the delights the Saviour has in His beloved. A careful comparison of our findings indicates that He desires to find in us what the Holy Spirit is working to perfect in us. The one beautiful fruit of the ministry of the Holy Spirit in the Christian includes, "love, joy, peace, long-suffering, gentleness, goodness, faith, meekness, temperance" (Galatians 5:22-23). These link quite firmly in respective order with the teaching about the Shulamite's eyes, her teeth, her temples, her breasts, her neck, her lips, her locks, her hair, and her speech.

For the shepherd there was a joy in loving the maiden because she was exactly as he desired her. As the Holy Spirit develops His perfect fruit within us, we become intensely lovable to the Lord, who loved us when everything we were opposed Him, and should have repelled Him.

Knowing that circumstances will separate them again for a time, the shepherd promises to be as near as possible.

> *"Until the day break, and the shadows*
> *flee away, I will get me to the mountain*
> *of myrrh, and to the hill of*
> *frankincense"* (Song of Solomon 4:6).

The Shulamite once sent the shepherd to wait all night on the mountains of Bether. Now he promises to be out on the mountains at night, but the location is different.

Myrrh and frankincense were used in the temple activities. Frankincense was offered with the meal offerings upon the brasen altar. The meal offering would burn up in just a few minutes, but the frankincense burned on and on, being exceptionally fragrant. Since the temple was a busy place full of activity, a large quantity of frankincense was burning on the altar all of the time.

He was promising to be in the mountains around Jerusalem, so that again he would be near her when she realized her danger. He uses the maiden's own words. The morning for which he waits is the time when the dark shadow of Solomon's influence upon her is gone forever, so that they can walk together without the evil king ever separating them again.

"Thou art all fair, my love; there is no spot in thee"   (Song of Solomon 4:7).

His final words share the joy he has in the Shulamite, while he reminds her that she has so far kept herself unspotted, even though she has often been weak.

Chapter 10

BUILD A BARRIER
TO TEMPTATION

The shepherd drops out of sight as Solomon dominates the scene, restless and ready for the journey. As always the conversation abounds with references to himself, who he is, and what he will do.

"Come with me," he says, swelling with self-importance and pride, using the name "spouse" to indicate that he is assured of victory as he reaches for her heart.

"Come with me from Lebanon, my spouse, with me from Lebanon: look from the top of Amana, from the top of Shenir and Hermon, from the lions' dens, from the mountains of the leopards"
(Song of Solomon 4:8).

The king elects to take the Shulamite on a sight-seeing tour of places that could only be explored by his majesty with plenty of protection from his own armed men. They climb in the chariot to some of the high areas, seeing lions' dens that his men have found, and the swift moving leopards. She has opportunity to see her own home town from a different angle than she has ever seen it before. The trip must have taken much planning and preparation, but Solomon was so anxious to dazzle the Shulamite that nothing was too much to do. No expense was too great. He wanted to fill her eyes with so many new and wonderful sights, that she would always look back on the trip as one of the great events of her life.

The great procession moves along. We hear snatches of conversation. The king is saying,

> *"Thou hast ravished my heart, my sister, my spouse; thou hast ravished my heart with one of thine eyes, with one chain of thy neck"*   (Song of Solomon 4:9).

The king had an unlimited scope of choice as he looked for companionship and love. It must have caused a flutter in the Shulamite's heart to know that he desired her.

Three factors are prominent in Solomon's conversation. Firstly, the king never forgets who he is. It is the king's heart that has been ravished by the maiden, and this is an item of no small consequence in the eyes of the king. He wishes her to understand clearly what a triumph this is for her. Secondly, he uses the term "spouse" again. He fully expects to ultimately capture her heart with his seduction. Finally, the basis of his attraction to her is unnatural and unreal. One of her eyes is appealing. What about the other? Of course this may mean one glance from her eyes, but even this is not enough to build love on. It might be enough to stir lust.

Her neck has an appeal only because of the necklace she is wearing. As always, it is the material glittering thing that is important to Solomon. He desires, not the Shulamite as she is, but the girl made beautiful by his expensive additions. His words are calculated to build a pride response; a feeling that she is better than the other girls he has met.

The king continues;

> *"How fair is thy love, my sister, my spouse! how much better is thy love than wine! and the smell of thine ointments than all spices! Thy lips, O my spouse, drop as the honey-comb: honey and milk are under thy tongue; and the smell of thy garments is like the smell of Lebanon"*
> (Song of Solomon 4:10-11).

Throughout the Song the word "beloved" is usually used to designate the shepherd lover. Coming from a verb that means "to boil" this title suitably depicts the constancy of the shepherd's love. He demonstrates this in the actions of love; caring, protecting, embracing, and adoring the person loved. The word "love" used here by Solomon is the same Hebrew word.

He was really saying, "How beautiful is your fervent love in action!" He had never seen her on fire with a love response. He was making an appeal to her human nature, knowing that everyone needs to be desired for himself or herself alone. Solomon knew what he was saying was not true but he felt that it would please her to hear it. He was acting on the level of Satan's appeal to the flesh, that old corrupt nature, still resident within the Christian.

Solomon exposes the true nature of his approach. He does not stay with truth, for he speaks of a boiling love of which he has not seen any evidence in the Shulamite. He quotes the girl's words from an earlier conversation saying that her love is "better than wine," to catch her ear. Then he tells her that it is her perfume he likes, and follows with a reference to her conversation, although she apparently has not said a word. He goes on to use a simile that he applies in Proverbs 5:3 to a harlot.

Solomon's whole approach is to the senses, with the accent on sweetness in experience, taste, and smell. The appeal is linked with the old nature that craves new sense experiences.

A parallel of the triple appeal Solomon made is outlined by John in his epistle; "For all that is in the world, the lust of the flesh, and the lust of the eyes, and the pride of life, is not of the Father, but is of the world" (1 John 2:16). This is all that is in the world according to the Scripture. The life that is lived out of fellowship with the Lord must be lived on the level of the lusting eyes, the lusting flesh, or the proud heart. John hastens to point out that the world is passing away, and so is the lust.

A day will come for the Christian when the lusting is all in the past. While it is here, Satan makes the supreme bid to use it to rob us of our fellowship with the Shepherd, and to completely spoil the joy that He could have in our lives day by day.

Solomon begins to realize that the Shulamite is different from the other girls who were so easily swayed by his proposals. He speaks of her as a garden, a spring, and a fountain, but in her relationship to him he has to confess that he has not reached her.

> *"A garden inclosed is my sister, my spouse; a spring shut up, a fountain sealed"* (Song of Solomon 4:12).

The word for garden literally means a fenced garden. Inclosing has the idea of fastening it closed, as though the entrance to the garden had been closed, secured and locked.

God originally prepared a garden in Eden so that He could have fellowship with man in a place that was a gift from God to possess and enjoy. It is the garden within the girl that is important to us. The garden with the growth, the beauty, the rest, and the potential for fellowship, is the heart of the maiden. There was nothing in the garden of her heart for Solomon. He was on the outside. The gate was closed to him.

This is a true picture of Bible separation. Much teaching is given about separation in the Christian life that is centred on things, situations, and kinds of people. The true separation is heart separation. The Scripture speaks of the Lord Jesus as being, "separate from sinners" (Hebrews 7:26), yet we read the report of eye-witnesses who said of

Him, "This man receiveth sinners, and eateth with them" (Luke 15:2). Separation did not stop the Lord Jesus from mixing with sinners, or for caring for them in a personal, tangible, and loving way. Rather it meant that there was nothing in His heart that belonged to, or gave pleasure to Satan.

The disciples learned this lesson from the Master. In their own ministry we find the evidence of it. After the Holy Spirit came, they were witnesses of Jesus to the people of their generation. They did not cluster together with other Christians, and send notices to the unbelievers in their communities that the good news would be preached at a certain hour. They went back into the very buildings where the errors of traditional Judaism had been propagated. To the very people who taught error, they proclaimed truth, "continuing daily with one accord in the temple" (Acts 2:46). They were separated unto the Lord in their hearts. Physically they mingled with the unbelievers to reach them with the glorious gospel of Christ.

The word for "inclosed," in reference to the garden, is translated shut up as it relates to the spring. The maiden is like a spring with the pure water bubbling up, but this is closed off from the defiled and defiling king. She is like a fountain, but the king has found her to be sealed. Nothing pours from her life for his enjoyment.

Though they were sitting side by side in the royal chariot, she was separated from him in the truest sense. There is nothing in the Shulamite's heart which the king can enjoy, but he does see fruit in her life. He speaks of the fruit he recognizes:

"Thy plants are an orchard of pomegranates,
with pleasant fruits; camphire, with spikenard,
spikenard and saffron; calamus and cinnamon,
with all trees of frankincense; myrrh and aloes,
with all the chief spices"

(Song of Solomon 4:13-14).

The king does not have insight into what makes the Shulamite tick, as the shepherd does. He looks on her from an objective position. What he sees in her would be comparable with what the world sees in the Christian. She is an unusual person with a hidden inner resource he does not understand.

Remember that the shepherd saw nine dimensions of beauty in the girl, and the fruit of the Spirit has nine sides to it. The king mentions nine fruits in her garden by name. What the world sees is the fruit of the Spirit in our lives.

The fruits mentioned by the king are linked with taste, sight, and smell. The pomegranate makes good eating, while the cinnamon alters the taste of any mix in which it is included. The camphire and saffron were used as dyes, and all the spices had a powerful fragrance. The world can only tell what is real in our lives as they detect it by natural perception.

Paul had this in mind when he wrote that God's leading would enable us to "make manifest," or visible, the savour of the knowledge of Christ (2 Corinthians 2:14). The world, seeing us, should be able to read Christ in the way we live, act, and react. Paul expanded the truth by adding: "Ye are manifestly declared to be the epistle of Christ ministered by us, written not with ink, but with the Spirit of the living God; not in tables of stone, but in fleshy tables of the heart" (2 Corinthians 3:3). God, the Holy Spirit, writes the will of God upon our hearts. The onlooking world reads it in the witness of our lives.

The king began to see the Shulamite as:

"A fountain of gardens, a well of living waters, and streams from Lebanon" (Song of Solomon 4:15).

Water is essential for growth in any garden. Without water everything suffers. The king sees the bride as a "fountain of gardens." He understood that because the girl was closed off from him, and from his evil intent, her life overflowed with strength as from a hidden spring. This strength, he knew, could overflow into other lives. She would be able to nourish and bless the hearts of others. The source of this spring of love and life was the shepherd. His love flowed through her affecting everything she did.

The Lord is the source of our inner springs. The sons of Korah sang, "All my fountains are in thee" (Psalm 87:7). This is how it must be with us. Everything we need for life begins with Christ, and ends with Him. He is more abundant toward us than we could ever have expected. There is a continual overflow as we allow Him to fill us with His love.

The Garden of Eden had only one river running into it. God made the provision so that the Garden would be well watered and growth would be abundant. Yet, after the river had met all the needs of the Garden, there was not one river, but four, going out of Eden.

This is how the Lord still works. If we draw from Him the love we need, the result will be a multiplying of the waters that satisfy our own hearts. There will be a fountain of gardens in our lives that will nurture those around us. We will be channels for the blessing of the Lord into other lives.

The fountain, the well, and the stream present three different concepts about the Christian. A fountain is closely allied to a spring, having existence at and beyond its point of entry from the earth. The well exists only because it has been dug by someone, the water filling in the pit that was dug, but in this case filling it with living water, neither stagnant nor still. The stream flows from a higher place, and is of value as it passes, maintaining the water table which fills the well, and which keeps the spring pushing up.

We need to see all three dimensions in our lives. The flowing stream from the Lord keeps all our needs satisfied as it is received and allowed to work within us. The stream will not dry up, for it is, "the river of God, which is full of water" (Psalm 65:9).

Just as the well has to be emptied of earth before it can become filled with water, we need to be emptied of self before God can fill us. The water table will always be there, ready to fill, where an act of the will has made a man empty for God.

Finally, God will pour His life-sustaining moisture through us as abundantly as we allow Him to do it. We have the potential to be fountains. Conditions underlie the fountain experience, of course. We must be saved to share the water of life with another person. We must be taught in the Word before we can teach it, and we must be yielded to the Holy Spirit before He will use us as channels of God.

Jesus explained to the woman at the well, "Whosoever drinketh of the water that I shall give him shall never thirst; but the water that I shall give him shall be in him a well of water springing up into everlasting life" (John 4:14).

Later He called to the people of Israel on one of their feast days saying: "If any man thirst, let him come unto me, and drink. He that believeth on me, as the scripture hath said, out of his belly shall flow rivers of living water" (John 7:37-38). He linked this with the ministry of the Holy Spirit. The Lord planned to make a fountain of living water out of every one of us.

Solomon could see the aliveness in the maid from Shunem, but he knew that no part of this was available to him. He was out of it—so far. It was a great victory for the shepherd.

Chapter 11

BE LOVABLE

The ride to Jerusalem is over. No indication is given of the time lapse since the Shulamite and shepherd last met. The girl has long since made her decision that she will return the love of the shepherd, and longs to share this with him. She is willing for any experience as long as he knows for sure that she is now his and his alone.

She calls for the north wind to awake as though it has been sleeping. The north wind is often represented as a severe wind. In the book of Proverbs we are told that it, "driveth away rain" (Proverbs 25:23), and thus picture the powerful wind from the north, driving the clouds before it, drying the land as it passes, leaving its chill over everything.

"Awake, O north wind; and come, thou south; blow upon my garden, that the

*spices thereof may flow out. Let my
beloved come into his garden, and eat his
pleasant fruits"* (Song of Solomon 4:16).

In her longing for him she is willing for anything to happen so that he will know. She calls for
the north wind to blow into the garden of her heart
if that is what is necessary. She will go through an
even greater trial than she has had, if this will
bring them together. Judgment often comes from
the north. It may be that she is so aware of her un-
worthiness, in contrast to the excellencies of the
shepherd, that she is willing to suffer, if only this
separation will end. The shepherd has become more
important to her than any other living person.

The south wind is gentle. While the brisk
north wind builds the roots of growing plants, the
relaxed motion of the south wind aids in moving
pollen from plant to plant so that reproduction is
accomplished. The south wind, warm and full of
moisture from the Red Sea, aided early growth and
development. Job remarked that God "quieteth the
earth by the south wind" (Job 37:17). During
Paul's journey to Rome, we are told that "the
south wind blew softly" (Acts 27:13).

The opposing influences of north and south
winds are invoked by the Shulamite to come into
her garden so that the spices she knows are there
will flow out. When we know the things that delight the Lord have been developed within our
hearts, we begin to feel as she does. We want Him
to enjoy the fruit that He has formed within us.

The ownership of the garden seems to change
in her thinking once it is completely opened up to
the beloved. The winds are invited to blow into

"my garden," but once all the barriers are down and the invitation is given, it becomes "his garden."

More than anything else, the Lord desires to possess my heart. It was this that took Him to the cross, for Paul teaches that He "died for us, that, whether we wake or sleep, we should live together with him" (1 Thessalonians 5:10).

It was Paul's knowledge of this truth that caused him to pray as he did for the Ephesians: "That Christ may dwell in your hearts by faith" (Ephesians 3:17). Many of the Christians were missing the delight of having Christ dwelling within, as in His own home, for that is what the word "dwell" implies.

The Shulamite says, "Let my beloved come in. . . ." She knows that the garden will please the beloved. The things he likes are there: the spices, and his pleasant fruits. When we know that there is nothing in our hearts to which the Lord objects, we can really offer Him the possession of our inward man. If we have something hidden there that displeases Him, we will be willing to settle for a less intimate relationship with Him. In consequence, we will miss the true excitement of the life which He has given us. At the same time, the loss to our Beloved is great.

Her invitation is immediately accepted with the response of joy. "I am come in. . . ," he answers. While the depth of meaning of words between two real people is hidden within their own hearts, the Holy Spirit has left here an inventory of things that delight the Lord when they are found in our hearts.

"I am come into my garden, my sister, my spouse: I have gathered my myrrh with my spice; I have eaten my honey-comb with my honey; I have drunk my wine with my milk: eat, O friends; drink, yea, drink abundantly, O beloved" (Song of Solomon 5:1).

Once the heart has really been given to the Lord, He possesses it with delight. Everything in it belongs to Him as indicated by the repeated use of the personal pronoun. It is "my myrrh," "my spice," "my honey-comb," "my honey," "my wine," and "my milk." He is excited with what He finds there, but His great joy is that it has been committed to Him as His own. There are now no closed doors in the inner man refusing Him admission, no secret chambers with barriers sealing them off.

The Christian knows that the things the Lord desires to find in him have been put there by the inward ministry of God's Spirit.

Myrrh is one of the spices specially mentioned. One thing that will always be present in the Christ reflecting Christian is an appreciation of Christ's suffering and death. Myrrh is gathered from a pierced tree, and is a reminder of His suffering. Its bitter taste points to the bitterness of the cross, and His association with our guilt. The Lord left the feast with the loaf and cup to remember Him in His sacrificial rejection and pain, so that we might enjoy Him in the glory and beauty of His resurrection life.

Honey is gathered from the honey-comb, where it is put by its maker, the bee. Linking both together puts product and source as a unit.

There was a sweetness in the life of Christ which made Him unique among men during His life on earth. Humanity had long since gone sour, denying God's right to direct human affairs and to judge sins. The Lord Jesus came on the scene with a life that kept the ancient law in every detail, bringing glory from it, rather than rejection and judgment. The honey-comb from which this sweetness emanated was His tremendous desire to please the Father. He said to the disciples: "My meat is to do the will of Him that sent me, and to finish his work" (John 4:34), and to the Jews: "I seek not mine own will, but the will of the Father which hath sent me" (John 5:30).

His success in this is now a matter of history. At the time of His baptism, and again on the mount of transfiguration, God spoke audibly from heaven; first to declare that His Son pleased Him, and later to announce His right to be heard. Just before the events at Calvary, the Father spoke personally to the Son, claiming that He had glorified His name in the life of His Son, and that He would again glorify it in the death He would die: "I have both glorified it, and will glorify it again" (John 12:28).

The Son was sent to do the will of His Father. The honey-comb may represent His intent to do this: the sweetness of His life, the outcome of that desire. The honey and the honey-comb are found in the heart of the maiden, who represents us. This becomes a key to our understanding as we remember the words of the Lord, "As my Father hath sent me, even so send I you" (John 20:21). The Lord desires to find in us the same commitment to do His will that He had to do the Father's will.

Milk and wine have different meanings in Scripture. Milk represents the Word of God—"desire the sincere milk of the Lord" (1 Peter 2:2)—and wine speaks of joy in the heart of man according to Psalm 104:14-15: "He causeth the grass to grow for the cattle, and herb for the service of man: that he may bring forth food out of the earth; and wine that maketh glad the heart of man, and oil to make his face shine, and bread which strengtheneth man's heart."

The Bible references to wine consider its use as food in moderation in Bible land culture, but takes a strong stand against drunkenness. However, when we link the sacred Word and joy as the beloved links milk and wine, we instantly react knowing that the application of the Word of God does not always give joy. Often the Word will have a crushing effect, as we could discover sin and failure through the illumination it gives.

The unmentioned tie between the two is obedience. In His teaching to the disciples at the last supper, the Lord made a profound statement: "If ye know these things, happy are ye if ye do them" (John 13:17). The Word of God brings joy to the person who obeys. This is suggested to us by the linking of the milk and wine. The Lord finds His Word in the surrounded heart, but He also finds the joy of submission and response to Divine instruction.

As our Beloved takes possession of our hearts, He engages in joyous activity. He gathers the spice; He plucks or picks it as fruit. He eats the honey, but this word is used in reference to a banquet. It is the word used when Adam and Eve are told that they may "freely eat" of the trees of the

Garden of Eden. He drinks the wine and milk as though with relish and delight.

There is an excitement in the whole experience for Him. The cause of His excitement is that His fragrance has permeated the Christian's heart: His will is its guide; His Word its delight; and the joy of obedience tells that this heart has been caught by His love.

Delighted with what He has found, the Shepherd Beloved of our souls calls out: "Eat, O friends; drink, yea, drink abundantly, O beloved."

He has so enjoyed the garden—the yielded heart—so full of everything He values, that He now purposes to share what has become so precious to Him. Others are invited to come near because the heart He has filled is overflowing. Other lives will be fed from the overflow.

This is how we recognize the person who lives close to the Lord. His life has a spillover in which others who walk with the Master will find strength. The Lord invites those who are His friends to be nourished by those who satisfy Him.

This is the only time the girl is given the shepherd's title. She has become like him. The things that are valued by him are now her great interest. In this she portrays for us the person who has become like the Lord on the inside, with none of the trappings of pretended spirituality. This Christian is for real.

He calls her "beloved," but he knows that this will last only as long as she continues to draw all of her resources from him. She must "drink abundantly" of him.

And we must drink of Christ to remain like Him.

Chapter 12

IT'S TIME TO WAKE UP

Somewhere in the city of Jerusalem the Shulamite lay asleep. The room she slept in had its private entrance from the outdoors, but the girl slept, without fear, the heavy slumber that blots out all contact with the surrounding world. She is completely oblivious to the man who stands in the shadows, gently calling her name. The couple who had enjoyed such perfect love in the previous verse, are now out of touch with each other.

The Holy Spirit uses the incident to teach us a great truth: that the aftermath of a spiritual victory, or a glorious triumph in Christ, will be continuing joy only as we keep on drawing all of our resources from Him. Satan will do everything in his power to spoil our relationship with the Lord. He just cannot stand to see God's people being blessed in spirit, and thrilled by the Man of Calvary.

Elijah challenged the prophets of Baal. Four

hundred and fifty of them stood against this one man who stood with God. During a whole day, he waited as they called on Baal to consume a prepared sacrifice. There was no answer from Baal. As evening approached, Elijah set up the Lord's altar which had fallen into disuse, dug a trench around it, and filled the trench with water, soaking both the sacrifice and wood.

Elijah prayed. Immediately, God sent fire to consume the sacrifice, wood, stones, and water in a powerful demonstration that He was the only true God, and that the people of Israel should worship Him alone. It was a mighty victory for the prophet of Jehovah.

The next day we would expect to find Elijah still jubilant over the triumph of Jehovah over Baal, but Satan has reached him. Instead, we find a discouraged, drooping man, sitting under a juniper tree in the wilderness, wishing that he could die. He was terrified by the threats of Jezebel.

Generations earlier, the nation of Israel had been given a total victory at Jericho. They were the instruments in God's hands as He punished the evil populace of the walled city. Satan caused one man, Achan, to steal from God. They failed at Ai, the next city. When they should have been joyful at the power of God with them, they were crushed: "the hearts of the people melted, and became as water" (Joshua 7:5). Be assured that the Devil will strive to duplicate this in our lives as we yield to the Lord and see Him do mighty things.

The Shulamite, while sleeping, was out of contact with the shepherd. She could not see him, or touch him, or go to him. She was asleep. For a long time, she could not hear his voice as he called in the night darkness. Nothing got through to her. There was no response from her as she slept.

The sleeping Christian is like this. He is not listening to the Lord, nor speaking to Him. All language in sleep is garbled and disconnected. He is not watching the Lord, nor following Him. He has no taste for the Lord, though he may dabble in religious things. The "spirit of slumber" (Romans 11:8) is defined by Paul as unseeing eyes and unhearing ears.

In Romans, Paul focuses our attention on the return of the Lord, and calls those who are sleeping to awaken: "Knowing the time, that now it is high time to awake out of sleep: for now is our salvation nearer than when we believed" (Romans 13:11). Our response to His call He equates to casting off the works of darkness. We cast off the works of darkness when we awake out of sleep.

A sleeper, dead to the world around him, is often most active in the dream world. When we are asleep toward the Lord, we may be wide awake and actively engaged in the material world, finding our pleasure and satisfaction there. Paul understood this, and encouraged the early Christians to wake up. He told them, "we are not of the night, nor of darkness. Therefore let us not sleep, as do others; but let us watch" (1 Thessalonians 5:5-6).

The separating sleep is not for the Christian who loves the Lord. Those who are asleep are missing daily fellowship with Him. It is a death-like sleep that robs of everything that the Lord wants us to enjoy on an hour-by-hour basis. The new life in Christ is for living. The Lord encourages us to throw off the drowsiness that smothers it, and promises that if we do He will give us light; He will shine upon us.

The Shulamite begins to be aware of the calling shepherd. "My heart waketh," she says.

It is in the heart that the awakening must take place: not in the muscles as we try to do more; not in the brain as we try to know more; nor in the lips with an effort to witness more. The Beloved reaches for the heart. Once this is truly His, everything else follows. To arouse the heart, the Beloved speaks. He knows that His voice will stir us as nothing else will.

The Shulamite slumbered until she heard the shepherd's voice. Even then her response was slow. The teaching of the Word of God is the greatest force for arousing the sleeping Christian. The voice of the living Lord is heard in the preaching of the Scriptures.

> *"I sleep, but my heart waketh: it is the voice of my beloved that knocketh, saying, Open to me, my sister, my love, my dove, my undefiled: for my head is filled with dew, and my locks with the drops of the night"* (Song of Solomon 5:2).

As the Lord speaks through His preachers, there is a Divine stirring in our hearts. We recognize His voice.

Haggai preached to the people of God who had returned from Babylon to Jerusalem fifteen years earlier to build the temple. As he looked around, he discovered that they all had beautiful homes and lands, but the temple project had hardly gotten off the ground. He began to preach about God's timing and God's vision of dwelling with His people. The Israelites began slowly to respond to this powerful teaching, having a desire to obey. "Then spoke Haggai, the Lord's messenger in the Lord's message unto the people, saying, I am with you, saith the Lord" (Haggai 1:13).

This caused a great stirring of the people. Zerubbabel, the governor, and Joshua, the high priest, shared in the experience. It was the inward stirring of their spirits by the Lord. The Holy Spirit uses a word which means, "to wake," and which contains the idea of opening the eyes. They had been going through the ritual of worship with their spiritual eyes closed, and had lost the vision God had for His remnant people.

Fifteen years before, Cyrus had had his eyes opened by the Lord and had sent them back to Jerusalem with wealth and spiritual vision. They had worked hard for a year. Then, like so many of us, they fell asleep, to be roused by the Lord under the preaching of Haggai. His word shook them awake. When they had awakened, the work was no longer tedious or distasteful. They could not wait to get to it. The Scripture record says, "They came and did work in the house of the Lord of hosts, their God" (Haggai 1:14).

The knocking voice of the shepherd stirred the Shulamite from her sleep. The first words she heard were, "Open to me," followed quickly by four favorite possessive names he had called her often in the past.

"My sister," refers to the friendship they had had in their own village, with a peer group, where they were all like brothers and sisters. They liked each other then. Even now, though they were lovers, that friendship was still intact.

"My love," refers to close association with a woman. The root of the word indicates tending or caring for a flock, suggesting a yoke they shared, as well as a tie that held their hearts together.

"My dove." Twice before in the song, the shepherd has mentioned that the maid had doves' eyes. We noted that the dove makes a peculiar wailing sound when alone, and seems always to be watching for its mate. He has also called her "a dove," when she was in danger from Solomon, yet hiding from the shepherd. Now he is sure she will be his, and calls her "my dove," even though the interaction between them is sluggish for the moment. He is her protector, and she has eyes for only him.

"My undefiled," could be rendered, "my perfect one." The thought is not that she has been made clean, but that she has stood apart from defilement because of him. She is a complete person, nothing having been sacrificed to sin. Paul applies the fullness of this truth to the Christian as he writes to the Colossians. He encouraged them to find Christ as the centre of their whole existence, then says, "and ye are complete in him" (Colossians 2:10).

There was good reason why the Shulamite should open to the shepherd. All the hours she had been sleeping, he had been outside calling for her to open. His protection had been available to her even in rejection. His care and attention had been directed toward her.

The dew falls as the darkness falls, so the shepherd began calling the Shulamite with the onset of night. In spite of the discomfort of the dew and wetness, he continued calling until he reached her. As long as the bride was in darkness and asleep, the shepherd kept calling.

Other friends of Solomon may have been sleeping in the same residence, but the shepherd called for the Shulamite alone. She was the one who had responded to his love. He saw her presence in that building as dangerous for her, and desired to enter that he might bring her out. Paul speaks for our Beloved in Ephesians 5:14; "Awake thou that sleepest, and arise from the dead, and Christ shall give thee light."

The Shulamite, partly aroused, saw many problems that kept her from running to the shepherd.

> "*I have put off my coat; how shall I put it on? I have washed my feet; how shall I defile them?*" (Song of Solomon 5:3)

To us they look like silly excuses. To her they were real obstacles because she was not wide awake. She could not see things clearly.

The Lord spoke to drowsy Christians in Laodicea. A comfortable, half-asleep feeling is suggested in their words, "I am rich, and increased with goods, and have need of nothing" (Revelation 3:17). The Lord tells it as it is: "And knowest not that thou art wretched, and miserable, and poor, and blind, and naked." The Christians felt comfortable in their lethargy. Non-Christians in the congregation saw nothing in the others to disturb them or to make them feel they were out of it.

The Lord was knocking on the hearts of these people so that they would be awakened to their loss of fellowship with Him. He wanted to open their eyes so that they would see Him as He really was. Their blindness would respond to His eye-salve. He says, "I counsel thee ... anoint thine eyes with eye-salve, that thou mayest see" (Revelation 3:18).

They needed to hear His voice, and willingly open the doors of their lives to Him. No longer would they feel comfortable away from His fellowship.

The well-known invitation is spoken by the voice of the Beloved: "Behold, I stand at the door, and knock: if any man hear my voice, and open the door, I will come in to him, and will sup with him, and he with me" (Revelation 3:20). All the Lord needs from us is the open door into our lives. He will then enter in and fellowship with us, knowing that before long we will be active and alive in our fellowship with Him.

What was missing in the Shulamite was this active response. She had no question that he was "my beloved," to her, and she was interested in drowsily listening to his voice. It was the active response that was absent; the movement toward him that should have left nothing between.

She listened, partly to him, and partly to herself as that inner voice told her that there were many good reasons why she could not rise and go to the door. Then she opened her eyes and saw the hand of the shepherd:

"My beloved put in his hand by the hole
of the door, and my bowels were moved

for him. I rose up to open to my beloved;
and my hands dropped with myrrh, and
my fingers with sweet-smelling myrrh,
upon the handles of the lock" (Song of
Solomon 5:4-5).

All at once the problems about rising in the
night are gone. She sees him. The mist of sleep
lifts. Her heart is moved for him, for that is what
the word "bowels" intends. Without hesitation, she
moves to open the door.

The hand of her beloved made the difference.
That hand had steadied her as she walked the
rough shepherd trails. Its strength had helped her
at times when her strength had not been sufficient.
The caress of that hand had stirred her in a way
she had not thought possible.

The door was locked from the inside. She
must open it. Very likely the shepherd could have
reached in from the outside, but he would not force
her to receive him.

She opened the lock, and immediately felt the
liquid myrrh on her fingers. She understood its
message. The rejected lover had reached his hand
through the opening in the door to put liquid
myrrh on the lock, so that she would not think his
love had changed. It was a custom to do this in her
land. When a suitor got no response to his call at
the door of his loved one, he would cover the lock
or bolt of the door with sweet-smelling ointment to
show his disappointment.

The unchanging love of the Lord is seen in
this. While we may separate ourselves from Him
by our coldness or our sin, we cannot separate ourselves from His love. "Who shall separate us from

the love of Christ?" (Romans 8:35), asks Paul. Among the other things that he lists, he includes life, and things present. The life that I live may separate me from Christ, but never from His love. Present things may claim my attention, and draw me away from Him, but His love will continue. I belong to Him. He is pledged to love me.

> *"I opened to my beloved; but my be-loved had withdrawn himself, and was gone: my soul failed when he spake: I sought him, but I could not find him; I called him, but he gave me no answer"*
> (Song of Solomon 5:6).

He was gone! With hands still moist and fragrant with his myrrh, she realizes that she waited too long. The opportunity to go with the man she loves has been lost, not because she did not love him, but because her response to his love had been made sluggish by sleep.

The disciples had a comparable experience in the garden of Gethsemane. The Lord sat in the garden. He had wept and talked with His Father but that was now over. He is waiting now, aware that the crowd has already left the city, and is moving toward the Mount of Olives. His disciples are close by, but they are not excited about this quiet time with Him. They are fast asleep. Close as they are, they do not hear a word He is saying.

During these moments, the Lord made two tremendous statements: "The hour is come," and "Behold, the Son of Man is betrayed into the hands of sinners" (Mark 14:41). The disciples neither saw nor heard. Because of sleep, they missed it. In just a few hours Jesus' body would be mutilated and broken in death.

The time for the Bride's response was while he was speaking. That was when her soul failed her. The soul is the centre of the reason, emotions, and will. Within the soul she should have recognized her beloved's voice. Then she should have let her emotions respond to it. She should have opened to him, so that he could have taken her home again. The failure to respond began in her soul.

That is how it was with Jonah. God spoke to this man who had previously served Him. Outwardly, Jonah looked good but there was failure in his soul. He understood the command of God, but had no positive emotional response to it. What he willed to do was directly opposed to God's plan for him. He moved away from God, down to Joppa, down into the ship, and then down into the hold of the ship. It was three days later that the failing soul finally gave up, and called out to the Lord. Jonah tells us, "When my soul fainted within me, I remembered the Lord" (Jonah 2:7).

The Shulamite realizes what she has done, and steps through the open door to find her beloved. He may have been forced to leave by the approach of the watchmen. She calls in the darkness, but there is no answering response from the shepherd. Though she searches fervently, she does not find him.

> 'The watchmen that went about the city
> found me, they smote me, they wounded
> me; the keepers of the walls took away my
> veil from me"   (Song of Solomon 5:7).

A new group of watchmen now find the Shulamite. She is in a different city from her last encounter with the protectors of the people. Success for the watchmen means safety for the people of the city from danger in the night.

An exceptional watchman would take individual interest in a person in trouble, and try to help, but human nature makes a job out of the highest calling. No inquiry seems to have been made. On circumstantial evidence alone, the girl is suspect. She looks like a prostitute walking the streets in the night calling for a man she cannot find.

She is dealt with accordingly. When she receives the blows from the striking watchmen, wounds are made which may leave scars. The keepers then steal her veil. She stumbles on in the night, hurting, and exposed.

The watchman who is appointed by God has a ministry of words, not wounds. God appointed Ezekiel as a watchman to "warn the wicked of his way to turn from it" (Ezekiel 33:9). If the house of Israel rejected the watchman's words, he had no further responsibility. They would die because they refused the warning of the Lord.

The elder or overseer in the New Testament has a watching ministry. "They watch for your souls, as they that must give account" (Hebrews 13:17). Paul explained to Titus that the elder must have self-control. He must not be the kind of person who would strike another. His work was to hold fast to the Scriptures, learning Bible truth himself "that he may be able by sound doctrine both to exhort and to convince . . ." (Titus 1:9).

The tendency to rule others with vigour may cause the elder to be very severe in the execution of his office. Peter understood this human frailty, and so explained to his fellow elders that they were not to lord it over other Christians: "Neither as being lords over God's heritage, but being ensamples to the flock" (1 Peter 5:3). No mandate is given to the servant of God to damage one of God's children. His ministry is to help, not hurt.

The Shulamite stumbles on with neither comfort nor care from the men who should have been concerned about her. They abandon her to the dangers of the city and return to their pretense of watching over the sleepers.

Chapter 13

SEE THE BEST
IN YOUR LOVER

The night search fails. Discouraged, the Shulamite returns to her apartment, keenly aware that the separation between the shepherd and herself is her own doing.

Her first contacts in the morning are with some of the harem, the daughters of Jerusalem. She pours out her grief, and pleads with them to convey a message to her beloved if they see him. She forgets that they have not ever seen him. They do not know who he is. In her intense concern, she feels that everyone should be looking for him.

> *"I charge you, O daughters of Jerusalem,*
> *if ye find my beloved, that ye tell him, that*
> *I am sick of love"* (Song of Solomon 5:8).

The message that she asks them to share is not one which would be easy for a woman to discuss with a total stranger. She wants the rebuffed shepherd to know that she loves him so much that she is physically ill because of the estrangement she has caused.

The harem women respond with a question:

> *"What is thy beloved more than another beloved, O thou fairest among women? What is thy beloved more than another beloved, that thou dost so charge us?"*
> (Song of Solomon 5:9).

The women are puzzled. They have watched the Shulamite and have found her to be an exceptional girl, winsome in appearance and behaviour. They do not understand her kind of person, but they still rate her "fairest among women." Her distress about a missing lover, who is an obscure, unimportant person, is a mystery to them. Solomon is their man. He could be hers. Who could compare to the king?

They want to know what it is about the shepherd that makes him so special that she would enlist their help to find him.

The Shulamite responds as a girl in love. She tells why the man she desires to marry means so much to her.

The Holy Spirit has woven into these words a description of the Lord Jesus Christ. They echo our feelings toward Him. Though at first they seem obscure, a little investigation will unearth much of the New Testament teaching about the Lord.

> *"My beloved is white and ruddy, the chiefest among ten thousand"* (Song of Solomon 5:10).

It seems like a contradiction to speak of a person being white and ruddy, or red, at the same time. The contrast of his fair skin to her dusky complexion was important to her, but she had seen him often in intense activity as a shepherd, with the flush of activity showing.

The word "white" means dazzling or sunny. It comes from a root word which contains the idea of being whiter, as though leading to ultimate whiteness. This kind of whiteness showed on the mount of transfiguration when the Lord allowed the three disciples to see the brilliance of His Divine glory. Mark says: "And his raiment became shining, exceeding white as snow; so as no fuller on earth can white them" (Mark 9:3).

In contrast, the word "ruddy" means to show blood or to flush, particularly in the face. It is from this Hebrew word that the name of the first man, Adam, comes. Adam simply means man.

Our Beloved is God and man. Everything that God is, He is. Yet from the moment we see Him, and for all eternity, He will be a man. Thomas discovered this. As he looked at the man who stood before him, he said, "My Lord and my God" (John 20:28). Paul taught it to Timothy in a letter he wrote. "Great is the mystery of godliness: God was manifested in the flesh ..." (1 Timothy 3:16). John rejoiced in it, "The Word was God" (John 1:1), he said "The Word was made flesh, and dwelt among us ..." (John 1:14).

As the Shulamite compared her shepherd with other men, she always favoured him. Though she should make ten thousand such comparisons, he would always rise above the rest. To her he is the "chiefest among ten thousand."

The word "chiefest" indicates setting up a banner, or raising a flag for the person because he is preeminent. In the eastern setting it was customary to have one person at a feast or celebration who was the chief ruler of the occasion. He was identified by a flag, a banner, or a canopy. It was the ruler of the wedding feast in Cana who commended the bridegroom for keeping the best wine to the last. The ruler had to be chosen, and this choice is indicated in the Hebrew. In the first translation of the Hebrew Scriptures into Greek, the words were rendered, "chosen out of, or from ten thousand."

The Lord Jesus Christ is the central person of our universe. All of the action centers around Him. He is the King of kings and Lord of lords, even though we do not always see this in evidence. The Father has chosen Him and has decided to so order the future, "that in all things he might have the preeminence" (Colossians 1:18). It is vital that He should be chosen by each of us to have the preeminent place in our lives. He will then become to us the chief among the tens of thousands.

> *"His head is as the most fine gold, his locks are bushy, and black as a raven"*
> (Song of Solomon 5:11).

We make a mistake if we take the Shulamite's description as though it referred to a still picture, or a sculpture of a person. It is the real shepherd she is describing; a man full of life with great capacity to share with her and to love her. As she mentions the head, she is not thinking only of his attractive profile, but also of his thoughts, and how his mind works.

The word for "gold" refers to the finest and purest gold. It includes in it the idea that it was found that way. Strong's Concordance makes the comment that it is gold that is "pure as originally mined," and it therefore refers to a gold nugget that has never been impure.

The Shulamite was speaking of the shepherd's thoughts and attitudes toward her.

We must also make the personal application. Look back through the centuries to creation and beyond. There has never been a time when the Son of God did not have love in His thoughts about us, or when He did not have a plan that would save us from ourselves and from the staining sins that would crowd into our lives. At the time of creation He said, "My delights were with the sons of men" (Proverbs 8:31). In every prophetic commitment to bless His people He had us in mind.

It is natural to want to be near the people we love. Jesus talked with His Father just before His trial and crucifixion, and we can read His thoughts in the prayer. "Father, I will that they also, whom thou hast given me be with me where I am" (John 17:24). Look into the future, and it is the same. The Lord Jesus will come to earth as King of kings to mightily judge and rule the nations. It will be a day of glory, of acceptance, of the triumph of good over evil. We would expect to be in the background of the Lord's thoughts when He has so much to do. But no! Paul was taught by the Holy Spirit that "he shall come to be glorified in his saints, and to be admired in all them that believe" (2 Thessalonians 1:10). The important thing in His mind will be that we should see Him as He is, and that our hearts should be stirred to wonder and admiration.

The shepherd's hair would not be shaped, styled, and combed to perfection. He was an active man. His hair would reflect the action. "Bushy" has reference to the trailing bough of a bush.

As the head and the hair are tied together in the description, so must the thoughts of a person be linked with his actions. The Lord links His right thoughts toward us with right actions. An evidence of this is presented by John. He teaches that the moment any Christian sins, his Advocate deals with that sin in heaven. As the accuser points the finger at the sinning saint, the Lord Jesus steps forward to declare that He has already paid the cost of that sin on the cross. He then waits for us to confess the sin, so that He can forgive it, and restore our full fellowship with Him.

He is also active in His ministry as High Priest, and as the chief Shepherd. He also meets with His people whenever they gather together. This present activity of the Lord makes Him most precious to His bride. The black color suggests youthful vigour.

> *"His eyes are as the eyes of doves by the rivers of waters, washed with milk, and fitly set"*   (Song of Solomon 5:12).

The lovely Shulamite had looked into the eyes of her shepherd. They were the steady warm loving eyes that told her he cared. Full of expression, they focused perfectly on her, and poured out without words the message of his love. His eyes had lustre and life. They were like fountains.

In fact, the word she uses is often used to indicate a fountain in the Bible. Strong says that it refers to the fountain as "the eye of the landscape." Since the fountain pours out, we must think of the output of the eyes of the beloved. He has spoken before of her eyes as doves' eyes. An added dimension of truth is found here. Both the English and the American revisers considered it more accurate to compare the eyes of the beloved to doves, rather than to doves' eyes.

The word for dove has built into it the idea of warmth. The eyes of the beloved poured out the warmth of his love. The Shulamite knew that love was directed toward her.

Peter had denied the Lord three times, cursing, lying, and losing his temper. Then he saw the rejected Lord Jesus look his way. The warmth and love were still in the eyes of the man he had denied. It broke Peter's heart. We see him sobbing in the night. Even after he was aware of the watching eye of the Lord, and later wrote, "The eyes of the Lord are over the righteous" (1 Peter 3:12).

The Lord's love is in His eyes, but we are imperfect still. He shed tears because of human failure while on earth at the tomb of Lazarus, and on the final approach to Jerusalem just before His crucifixion. Isaiah prophesied that He would be known as "a man of sorrows and acquainted with grief" (Isaiah 53:3). We often grieve Him, and though He will one day wipe away all tears, His eyes are as doves beside the waterbrooks. The tears are often near because His love is so great and ours so fickle.

As the Christian faces his Lord, he becomes aware that His eyes miss nothing. There is no imperfection in Christ, no cross vision, no uncertain image. His eyes are fitly set. Even the white of the eye tells of this. White as though washed with milk, with no hint of infection, strain or redness, the perfection of His eyes tells that He has seen everything. The glistening of a tear only emphasizes that what He has seen has not turned His heart away from us. He still loves, and desires.

> *"His cheeks are as a bed of spices, as sweet flowers; his lips like lilies, dropping sweet-smelling myrrh"* (Song of Solomon 5:13).

Both the spices and the flowers give an enjoyable fragrance. They change the whole atmosphere around them. Many of the spices could also be added to food, and would change the taste of the whole dish.

The word "cheeks" used by the Shulamite carries the idea of softness. Without doubt she spoke of the shepherd with memories of a loving embrace when they stood cheek to cheek.

Time after time in the Bible, the cheek is linked with violence. Men struck their enemies on the cheek, and thus humiliated them. The normal reaction was an immediate counterattack. The Lord Jesus had the added suffering of plucking out the hairs of His beard, and they spat on His face.

Christ never retaliated. There was no counterattack from Him. At the sting of each slap, the love of the Saviour reached out to the striker.

We can see the counterpart to the tenderness of the embrace in the Lord's response. There was no hardness in Him, but rather a pity for failing

man, a tender longing for his soul. James speaks of
this, "The Lord is very pitiful, and of tender
mercy" (James 5:11). The tenderness of the
Lord adds its fragrance to everything we share with
Him. To have Him dwell within and possess us, we
must have a heart like His. He repeats His appeal
three times in the New Testament, "Harden not
your hearts..." (Hebrews 3:8, 3:15, 4:7).

The lips, in contrast, are active, not passive,
and the word "dropping" is elsewhere translated
"prophesy." It is the words of the speaking lips of
the beloved that stir the Shulamite to remember.
Recall that myrrh represents suffering. Many of the
prophetic words that dropped from the lips of the
Lord Jesus during His earthly ministry told of suffering.

He said to His disciples, "I am the good shepherd: the good shepherd giveth his life for the
sheep... As the Father knoweth me, even so know
I the Father: and I lay down my life for the
sheep" (John 10:11, 15).

Before the last supper, He said, "With desire I
have desired to eat this passover with you before I
suffer" (Luke 22:15). Mark tells us that: "He
began to teach them, that the Son of man must
suffer many things, and be rejected of the elders,
and of the chief priests, and scribes, and be killed,
and after three days rise again" (Mark 8:31).

He also quotes the Lord as saying, "It is written of the Son of man, that he must suffer many
things, and be set at nought" (Mark 9:12). These
words of his about suffering are precious to us. We
know that the suffering would have been left for us,
apart from His intervention at Calvary.

The beloved's lips are compared to lilies, but

the word appears elsewhere in the Bible almost untranslated—"shoshannim." It could have been translated "trumpet," and may refer to the use of trumpets in four psalms where it appears in the title. His lips are like trumpets which have a message for us. The dropping, or prophesying, continues.

Compare the psalms where the title "shoshannim" appears and the message is expanded. The first is Psalm 45. The psalmist writes of the Son of God as a truly beautiful person—"fairer than the children of men" (Psalm 45:2). He then tells of the striking beauty of the King's Son as He girds on His sword and rides into battle against lies, rebellion, and sin. He then tells of the beauty of the throne room, of the sceptre, of the coronation, and of the heavenly palace. It is the most thrilling description of God's greatest man. He is God's lily in His beauty.

Psalm 69 has "shoshannim" in the title, but here God's lily is crushed. It is the prophetic description of the suffering of the cross. The message of His lips as He calls out in the darkness is, "The reproaches of them that reproached thee are fallen upon me" (Psalm 69:9). This is a Messianic Psalm, and foretells the sufferings of Messiah. We can hear our Beloved from the cross speaking the words: "They that hate me without a cause are more than the hairs of mine head: they that would destroy me, being mine enemies wrongfully, are mighty: then I restored that which I took not away. . . . Reproach hath broken my heart, and I am full of heaviness: and I looked for some to take pity, but there was none; and for comforters, but I found none. They gave me also gall for my meat;

and in my thirst they gave me vinegar to drink" (Psalm 69:4, 20-21). The most beautiful man who ever lived was crushed upon the cross, while defiled and sinning men stood watching. God's lily was crushed under the load of human sin.

"Shoshannim" again appears in the title of the 80th Psalm, but here it is linked with a second word, "Eduth," which is not translated either. "Eduth" is the word that is sometimes translated testimony, in the extensive teaching of the tabernacle. The two words together present Christ as the "Lily of Testimony." In the days of Moses, the people gathered together with the "testimony," or the written law in their midst. We now gather around the living Word, the Lord Jesus Christ, who is the "Lily of Testimony." He was crushed and alone on the cross, but will never be crushed nor alone again.

All of the beauty of Christ is restored in His resurrection. Gathered around Him now are those who have responded to His love. They will ultimately show His full beauty in their lives, and even now begin to reflect Him. He is the "Shepherd of Israel," and the "Lord God of hosts." The fruit of His sacrifice is gathered around Him with one great desire filling their hearts: "Cause thy face to shine; and we shall be saved" (Psalm 80:19). They have been saved and gathered to Him. Now they wished to be saved from all else for His enjoyment.

Psalm 60 has the same words in the title, although the English spelling is altered slightly. Those who are gathered around the "Lily of Testimony" have had severe, disappointing experiences, which they know to be the result of disobeying the

Lord. They have come to understand His holiness
and to realize that when His people lose the beauty
of holiness, they also lose much of the benefit of
His fellowship. He is holy, and therefore must
stand always on holy ground. He maintains His
holiness through judgment. They refer to Him as,
"Thou, O God, which didst not go out with our
armies" (Psalm 60:10). Yet they return to Him
with the confidence that, "Through God we shall
do valiantly: for he it is that shall tread down our
enemies" (Psalm 60:12).

His lips, like lilies, or like trumpets, tell us
firstly of Himself, then of His suffering and death
for us, then of His desire to gather us close to Himself. Finally, they teach that this close fellowship
can only continue as we have holiness in our lives
as He has in His.

> *"His hands are as gold rings set with the
> beryl; his belly is as bright ivory overlaid
> with sapphires"*   (Song of Solomon 5:14).

The Shulamite describes the open hands of her
beloved, for that is what the word implies. It is the
open hand of our Beloved that shows the marks of
the cross.

She sets a high value upon his hands. They are
like gold to her. This is emphasized both by the
word she uses for gold, which is entirely different
from the word used earlier to describe his head,
and by the idea of the hands being "set with the
beryl."

The word for gold is used to describe the colour of oil in Zechariah 4:12, and is translated
"fair weather" in Job 37:22. Both looked like

gold. Pliny describes the beryl, or more accurately, chrysolithos, as "a transparent stone with a refulgence like that of gold." Here again is the gold-like appearance.

The beloved did not have hands that were golden to human sight, but they were golden to her inner sight. She placed great value on his hands. They had worked for her; had protected her; had caressed and embraced her, drawing her close to her beloved. His hands were infinitely precious to her.

Active hands are suggested by the word "rings," which is also used to describe the folding doors of the temple, and contains the idea of turning. The hands of our Beloved are precious in our eyes because of what He has done. As He now ministers to us, His hands turning in movement, the marks of the cross continually stir our hearts to greater love. We desire to feel His touch on our lives again and again.

At first thought, the description of the beloved's body sounds more like that of a piece of sculpture than of a real man. Here again we need to look below the surface.

The shepherd would often work in the heat with a minimum of clothing. The skin on his exposed body was always lighter than the Shulamite's, even when tanned. She uses the whiteness of ivory to express the contrast. His was a hard, muscular body, with no padding of fat. Blue veins showed on the bulging muscles, reminding her of the blue of sapphire.

There is more yet for the Christian who is looking for the excellencies of the Lord Jesus Christ. "Ivory" comes from a word that indicates the elephant's tusk, with the added thought of its sharpness, as though the emphasis was on the pointed quality of the ivory.

The body of the Lord Jesus Christ bears to this day, and for eternity, the mark of the tusk-like spear upon it. Thomas was invited to thrust his hand into that wound. This adds to the dimension of beauty we see in Christ.

To give depth to this thought, the word "sapphire" comes from a root word which means to score with a mark as a tally or record, according to Strong's Concordance. The words "scribe" and "writer" come from this root. The body of the Lord Jesus has been marked with stripes. He is quoted by one of the prophets as saying, "I gave my back to the smiters" (Isaiah 50:6). Many think the vicious scourging of the Saviour lies behind the words of Israel, "The plowers plowed upon my back: they made long their furrows" (Psalm 129:3). The marks of Calvary are marks of beauty to the Christian.

> *"His legs are as pillars of marble, set upon sockets of fine gold; his countenance is as Lebanon, excellent as the cedars"*
>   (Song of Solomon 5:15).

Marble pillars were on view in some of the great buildings of the ancient world, the grandeur of the marble being enhanced by the massive appearance of a row of giant columns. The shepherd had the powerful well-developed legs of a man in action, accustomed to travelling long distances on foot. To the Shulamite, they were beautiful because they were strong. Her security was linked with his strength.

The Lord "taketh not pleasure in the legs of a man" (Psalm 147:10), because He knows that when our strength feels adequate, we are often inclined to independence. In contrast, our pleasure in the Lord's strength shows that we have no illusions about our own need of a strength infinitely greater than our own. We need Him, and He is all we need.

The tabernacle pillars had stood in sockets of copper and silver, as though the sockets were feet that put the pillars in touch with a defiled world. The quality of gold is seen in the walk of the Beloved. Every step is pure, displaying the precious glory that is His.

Lebanon means "white." The name may have been given because the one hundred mile long mountain range has many snow-covered peaks, or because of the gleaming limestone cliffs. There is a parallel between this and the word "marble" in this verse which contains the idea of a bleached substance.

The Shulamite saw the lighter skinned man in contrast to herself, tanned and dark. To us the Holy Spirit gives the picture of the shadowless glory of the Beloved as so unlike us who, though redeemed and loved by Him, so often cast a shadow by turning.

Below the timberline, the cedars show a different kind of excellence. The cedars of Lebanon were the greatest in the world. These immense trees were used by Solomon in the building of the temple. The appearance of the evergreen beauty, the fragrance, the abundance of their growth, and the immensity, combined to make them the choice of all nations. The Shulamite is saying that her beloved is the choice one of all men. There is none to compare with him when the treasures of his personality are known.

> *"His mouth is most sweet; yea, he is altogether lovely. This is my beloved, and this is my friend, O daughters of Jerusalem"* (Song of Solomon 5:16).

The Shulamite almost bursts with desire and longing. She feels that she has failed her beloved. She finally speaks of his mouth. She wishes she could hear him speak to her as he so often had done. Everything about him is appealing to her. In the softened language of love, she can say of this most manly of men, "He is altogether lovely."

She calls him beloved, but the word "friend" tells us that she is sure her rejection of him during the night has not so alienated him as to spoil their relationship. He is still her friend.

We understand her feeling. So often, out of touch with our Beloved because of careless indifference, our inner self still claims His love, and trusts His faithfulness. Intuitively, not even admitting it, we know that even when we are faithless, "Yet he abideth faithful" (2 Timothy 2:13).

> *"Whither is thy beloved gone, O thou fairest among women? whither is thy beloved turned aside? that we may seek him with thee"* (Song of Solomon 6:1).

Caught by the Shulamite's description of the beloved, and by her obvious yearning for him, the daughters of Jerusalem now want to see him for themselves. They have not known men who warranted such description.

So it is with the Lord. When we speak about Him as He really is, His drawing power is felt by those who hear. They are caught by the witness of imperfect lovers, but are drawn by the true Lover to Himself. The Lord spoke of Calvary when He told His disciples that when He was lifted up from the earth, He would draw men to Himself.

Calvary is past. Now the believer is left with the privilege of lifting up the exalted Lord, so that the drawing power of the cross will be felt by all men.

Chapter 14

PUT IT INTO WORDS

The mystery suddenly clears in the girl's mind. She knows where the shepherd is! He is in his garden—the open spaces of the valley, where the lilies grow in such abundance. He had told her long before that if she ever needed to find him, he would be with the shepherds at the place where the flock was feeding.

> *"My beloved is gone down into his garden, to the beds of spices, to feed in the gardens, and to gather lilies"*
>   (Song of Solomon 6:2).

"His garden" contrasts with the luxurious gardens of the palace. The shepherd only has the valley pasture land, but that is what he enjoys. To him, this is familiar ground. He understands the vegetation—"spices"—and places a premium on the beautiful wild flowers. It is the kind of place where he rests easily, and where for years he has eaten his meals while watching the sheep.

The Christian does not need to remain away from communion with his Beloved. The Lord is as close to each of us as we will allow Him to be. It is our indifference to Him, or our involvement in sinful activities, that alienates Him. "Your sins have hid his face from you" (Isaiah 59:2).

"Give me your heart" (Proverbs 23:26), He pleads. This is the only way fellowship between us can continue unbroken. We give our hearts away, if not to Him, to some other person, pursuit or thing. The Lord tells it as it is. "Ye shall seek me, and find me, when ye shall search for me with all your heart" (Jeremiah 29:13). This promise still holds.

As she thought about the shepherd, and spoke about him, the Shulamite remembered where to find him. Our responses follow the same channels. As we think about Christ, we stir our love to Him into a flame. This love makes us want to obey Him. Our obedience brings us into His presence. We can be sure that He is near. He specifically promised that if we would obey Him out of love, then He would show us that He was near. John quotes Him as saying, "He that hath my commandments, and keepeth them, he it is that loveth me: and he that loveth me shall be loved of my Father, and I will love him, and will manifest myself to him" (John 14:21).

"I am my beloved's, and my beloved is mine: he feedeth among the lilies"
(Song of Solomon 6:3).

The girl used similar words earlier in the Song but her maturing love has caused a great change in her feelings.

"My beloved is mine," she had begun earlier. Now she begins, "I am my beloved's." She has changed the focus of her thoughts from what she possessed, to what she was willing to give. She could only be the beloved's if she gave herself to him. He had already given himself to her. Our Beloved has done the same for us. He waits for our willing response.

In both places she mentions that the shepherd feeds among the lilies, but her use of the knowledge is different. Earlier, she followed the comment by asking the shepherd to give her until morning to decide whether she would go with him or not. Now she hurries to the garden valley. The next words on record are the shepherd's as he speaks with her there.

We may be able to outline the Bible teaching about fellowship with Christ because we have an intelligent understanding of the principles involved. We need more than this. When our love to Christ is real, we will apply the principles; we will claim the experience of walking with Christ for ourselves.

> "*Thou art beautiful, O my love, as Tirzah, comely as Jerusalem, terrible as an army with banners*" (Song of Solomon 6:4).

These words of the shepherd were likely spoken to the Shulamite in the presence of the daughters of Jerusalem, who wanted to meet him.

It seems strange to think of comparing an extremely attractive girl to either a city or an army. The Holy Spirit teaches through the Song, without moving away from the knowledge and emotional responses of the people involved in it, who lived in ancient Israel.

As the shepherd travelled to Jerusalem, he passed Tirzah, a beautiful city, lying between Shunem and the nation's capital. Strong says the name of the city means delightsomeness. The city of Tirzah must have been a very pleasant and delightful place in Judea. One of the ancient Canaanite kings chose it for his residence.

Some think that Tirzah was located on a hill. It seems probable that the weary traveller, having come twenty miles from Shunem, would enjoy the view of the elevated town for some time before reaching it. This landmark would give him pleasure each time he passed.

He saw joy-inspiring beauty in the Shulamite as she unexpectedly approached him in the valley. It was the kind of beauty all who saw her could appreciate.

Jerusalem presents another side of her appeal to the shepherd. The most dazzling building in Jerusalem was the temple, centre of the worship of Jehovah. Beautiful on the outside, it was infinitely more glorious within. The glow of gold filled the interior. The veil, a vision of Divinely chosen colours, hung dead centre.

To the shepherd, the inward beauty of the Shulamite was priceless. To stress this he uses the word "comely" which means to be beautiful at home, where the inward self shows most easily.

The word "terrible" refers to a person whose

presence is commanding, requiring the attention of those who are near. One of the common descriptive terms applied by an eastern lover to his loved one means awe-inspiring. The onlooker was thought to be so impressed with the majesty of beauty, that he was struck with reverence for it, including intense respect and adoration.

The Lord sees in us an outward beauty in that we are not engaged in sin, but allow our inward faith to show in outward acts. The inward beauty is enjoyed by the Lord when He sees that there is no inward longing for forbidden sins.

The army with banners is not fighting, but it is making a mighty display of its power. The banners identify the allegiance of the troops. The Christian is strongest when he identifies powerfully with Christ, grasping the victory procured at Calvary by faith, rather than trying to win for himself what is already his to claim.

The sometimes uncertain Shulamite now identifies with her shepherd beloved. Her banners are waving.

> *"Turn away thine eyes from me, for they*
> *have overcome me: thy hair is as a flock*
> *of goats that appear from Gilead"* (Song
> of Solomon 6:5).

The shepherd repeats himself to the Shulamite. He has already shared in this delight with her. It was during a conversation that took place just before king Solomon took her in his car of state back to the city of Jerusalem. The maiden valued his repeated words just as we do. Repetition of the phrases of love becomes very precious to the person in love.

There is one very significant difference here. The daughters of Jerusalem are present. Does it not seem unusual to hear the shepherd express the most intense feelings in the presence of strangers?

He knew the daughters of Jerusalem were there. The words he spoke contained a message they needed to hear. They needed to understand that the pure love of one man for one woman was more precious than all the pomp and display of Solomon's palace, and the casual harem relationship with the king.

The words, "Turn away thine eyes from me," give a needed key to this passage. Throughout the Song, the shepherd has been appealing to the Shulamite to look on him alone, and to forget Solomon. Now that he has her absolute adoration, he directs her vision elsewhere.

The reason he gives is, "for they have overcome me," or as Strong indicates as a possible rendering, "for they have urged me." The open expression of love in her eyes toward him has stirred him to try to save others from the sick sadness of harem existence. This group of the daughters of Jerusalem may have been some of the "virgins without number" who could still get free.

Our Beloved says to us, "Lift up your eyes, and look on the fields; for they are white already to harvest" (John 4:35). These words were first spoken to those who followed Him, who had brought Him food, and were lovingly ministering to Him. He had become the centre of their existence. Now He got them to look on other men so that he could reach the others through these disciples.

The shepherd did not share everything he had said earlier to the Shulamite with the daughters of Jerusalem. There are areas of love that can only be expressed between lovers. The notable repetitions include reference to her hair, her teeth, and her temples.

Each of these has a practical application to our Christian responses. The hair suggests love's willing submission: the teeth, on display as in smiling, our joy: the temples, as the natural boundaries of our thinking mind put at rest by the Beloved, our peace. Love, joy, and peace are the first three facets of the fruit of the Spirit in Galatians 5:22. The Lord uses these as exhibits to the unconverted. They point to Him as the true Giver of life as man desires it. We are epistles, seen and read by others. The Lord uses our lives to turn men from the subtle deceptions of Satan.

> *"There are threescore queens, and fourscore concubines, and virgins without number. My dove, my undefiled is but one; she is the only one of her mother, she is the choice one of her that bare her. The daughters saw her, and blessed her; yea, the queens and the concubines, and they praised her"*
>
> (Song of Solomon 6:8-9).

The Shulamite is set apart from the queens, concubines, and virgins in the most definite and emphatic way. Solomon had sixty queens, eighty concubines, and unlimited virgins available for new sexual adventures, and he had only begun to depart from the Lord at this time. The record of the

Kings says: "But king Solomon loved many strange women, together with the daughter of Pharaoh, women of the Moabites, Ammonites, Edomites, Zidonians, and Hittites; Of the nations concerning which the Lord said unto the children of Israel, Ye shall not go in to them, neither shall they come in unto you: for surely they will turn away your heart after their gods. Solomon clave unto these in love. And he had 700 wives, princesses, and 300 concubines: and his wives turned away his heart" (1 Kings 11:1-3).

The Shulamite was distinctly separate from this great harem. She was "undefiled" according to our text. She stood alone, refusing the spiritual and moral defilment of the renegade king. It is this that makes the Song so unique. The man who penned the vanities of life in Ecclesiastes, tells of the love he never knew in the Song of Solomon.

Note the three groups involved in the king's women—queens, concubines, virgins.

The queens were linked to Solomon by the vows of marriage, were bearers of his true heirs, were known by his name, and could hold him responsible for their support. They could only be disposed of by divorce.

Concubines were also united to the king by a marriage ceremony, but were inferior in rank to wives, and could have no household authority. They had no rights through their form of marriage, except that they could legally engage in sexual intercourse with the man involved. They could be dismissed forever with a small gift. Their children had no claim on their father's estate, but had to be satisfied with any present the father might choose to give.

The virgins were women, gathered for Solomon's future pleasure, who had not yet been claimed by him, but who were willingly available.

The uniqueness of the Shulamite is emphasized as we compare her with the others. She had not been defiled by the king, nor did she plan any future defilement. She had not entered into any contract or agreement with him. Though she felt the pull of temptation, and had been unsteadied for a little, she had not yielded to the temptation.

She was the "choice one," or as another translator puts it, "the pure or clean one." The Lord values those who are willing to stand apart from others if that is necessary to the honour of His name.

"She is the only one of her mother," cannot mean that she was an only child, because we read of her mother's sons in the first chapter. The word "of" may indicate a likeness to her mother. A parallel thought is found in the New Testament. "They that are of Christ Jesus have crucified the flesh with the passions and lusts thereof" (Galatians 5:24 A.S.V.). Likeness to Christ will mean that we stand alone if we have to, but certainly separate from those who live on the level of the passions and lusts of the flesh.

The daughters of Jerusalem, queens, and concubines, all unite in noticing the difference so obvious in the Shulamite. They bless her and praise her because what they see in her, they admire and appreciate. The Lord advises us to follow her example. "Let your light so shine before men, that they may see your good works, and glorify your Father which is in heaven" (Matthew 5:16).

Chapter 15

WHO ARE YOU?

The daughters of Jerusalem are so moved by the shepherd's description of the Shulamite, and his one-to-one adoration of her, that they begin to look on her in a new light. They realize that they really do not know her. There is a light in her eyes that is missing from theirs. Though her complexion is dark, they can truly say that she "looketh forth as the morning." They recognize the radiance of her love, but cannot understand it.

> "Who is she that looketh forth as the morning, fair as the moon, clear as the sun, and terrible as an army with banners?" (Song of Solomon 6:10).

"Who is she?" they asked. As the moon glows against the dark sky, so she shines against the background of the empty gaiety and desolation of harem life, with a brilliance that has no basis of comparison in the other women. They know intuitively that if things were at their best, and light instead of darkness could represent the background of her life, she would still shine as the sun in the daytime sky. The pure, deep love in her life makes the difference. No surrounding circumstance can affect this.

Then they quote the shepherd in uncomprehending agreement—"terrible as an army with banners." This is the maiden that withstood the majesty and pageantry of Solomon. She now identifies only with the shepherd. All compromise is behind her. Their curiosity is overwhelming because they see beyond doubt that she knows who she is, and whose she is. They do not know what this is like, so she becomes an object of wonder to them.

"The world knoweth us not because it knew him not," says John (1 John 3:1). The Christian who loves the Lord Jesus with total abandon of self is a puzzle to the world, and equally an enigma to the carnal man or woman.

Many people in the Galatian church could not understand Paul's love for Christ that made him say, "I am crucified with Christ: nevertheless I live; yet not I, but Christ liveth in me" (Galatians 2:20). They were trying to please God by keeping part of the law; making the Christian men accept circumcision as it was practised in Israel. Paul kept pointing them to Christ, and telling them that the real and personal relationship they had with Him was what mattered. He finally pleaded: "Am I therefore become your enemy because I tell you the truth" (Galatians 4:16). Paul added that it was vital for the new creation to show in the lives of the Christians. He then stemmed the tide of critical opposition by saying, "I bear in my body the marks of the Lord Jesus" (Galatians 6:17). The Galatians knew about Paul's suffering as a missionary to the Gentiles. They knew that he had been scourged, stoned, and shipwrecked.

What Paul was saying went much deeper than this although many of them missed it. Jesus had put His marks on Paul's life because Paul had loved Him so much. The likeness of Christ was showing through Paul. He was already being changed from "glory to glory" (2 Corinthians 3:18). The Holy Spirit was moulding him into the image and likeness of the Christ he loved.

> "*I went down into the garden of nuts to see the fruits of the valley, and to see whether the vine flourished, and the pomegranates budded. Or ever I was aware, my soul made me like the chariots of Ammi-nadib*"
>
> (Song of Solomon 6:11-12).

The Shulamite began to tell them who she was—a simple maiden of Israel, making no claim to personal greatness or grandeur. Her interest in agriculture and growing things took her one day in the past into a valley close to her home. She had checked the garden where nuts were cultivated. Then she had walked on to see if the pomegranates were budding, or if the grape vines were sending out new shoots.

She was doing very ordinary things, but they were the things in which she found pleasure. The familiarity of her reference to both garden and valley suggest that she had been there many times before. She felt no threat of danger as she walked along unaccompanied. The open pasture land was most entrancing to her, causing her to daydream as she ambled along.

Suddenly, her reverie was broken by the appearance of Solomon's men. They apprehended her. Terrified, she had run with the swiftness of Amminadib's chariots. Her soul made her run. The fear from the inside, which we now know to be linked with body adrenaline, gave her the speed of fright, but there was no escaping the king's men. His majesty had ordered her brought to him.

The Christian can identify with the Shulamite walking alone in the valley, feeling so secure, yet surrounded by danger. Spirit hosts of evil surround the Christian wherever he goes. Safety for him depends on close fellowship with the Shepherd.

"Return, return, O Shulamite; return,
return, that we may look upon thee"
(Song of Solomon 6:13).

The daughters of Jerusalem are caught by the story, and by the unusual qualities they have discovered in the Shulamite. She stands in such contrast to the petty interests in harem life. She makes them aware of their own need, unknown until now—the need to be loved and cherished by one man, who responds to the love of one woman, and who cares for her and adores her above all others.

"Return," they pleaded. "Return, return." They desired to learn more from her. The little they have learned about the unknown person has made them long for more. They are stimulated by her realness, a most unusual quality in their circle.

Without doubt this is one of the great contributions the Christian can make. His life in Christ can create a vacuum in the hearts of others, as they discover the dimension of reality they have missed, being enjoyed by the Christian day by day.

Competition in harem life, with its wide spectrum of conflicts, had been the normal environment of the daughters of Jerusalem. The total difference of the Shulamite, non-conflicting, non-competitive, demonstrating the purest truest love they had ever seen, was refreshing. It causes them to wonder what makes her like this. They want to see more.

> *"What will ye see in the Shulamite? As it were the company of two armies"* (Song of Solomon 6:13).

The Shulamite asks the question. It seems unreal to her that the daughters of Jerusalem, surrounded by the sophisticated intrigues of the royal court, should want to see more of her. She could not understand their interest in her.

The Christian fails often to see the mystique of his life in the eyes of a world blinded to the beauties of Christ. Similarly, the Shulamite looked on her life as normal and usual. It was her simplicity, coupled with the power of her love to the shepherd, that held their attention.

There is some confusion about the exact translation of the answer given by the daughters of Jerusalem. It could be rendered, "as a dance before two armies," or, "dance of Mahanaim," or, "as at the dance of the two companies." The predominant idea is two armies, two companies, or two troops of dancers. They had seen the struggle of the true inner love, with the superficial love of things and circumstance. They wanted to consider this in greater depth.

The events of the Song took place during a forty year period in which no violent warfare took place in Israel. Their concept of war from experience consisted of handsome soldiers, perfectly trained, standing in their companies as associates in peace, without the horror of wounds or the stain of blood. The ravaging results of war were distant and unreal to them. Armies bred the idea of friendly competition. They did not seem too different from dancers.

The Shulamite had been torn by her inner warfare between two loves. To her it had been both real and violent. The whole thing had fascinated the daughters of Jerusalem, but they did not see it as a matter of life or death.

The Christian knows that the warfare is real. Flesh lusts against Spirit. Spirit lusts against flesh. The raging battle tears the Christian until in trusting love he claims the victory already won by Christ. Then peace rules through the power of God the Holy Spirit, who keeps the old sin nature in the place of death.

The evidence of the battle is seen by the surrounding world. Unbelievers watch the two armies without knowing what they see. The present relationship of the two armies is our present testimony. The world may consider it curious excitement, but to the Christian, it is the present battle of Calvary for his life; as vital and real as the historic battle of Calvary for his soul.

Chapter 16

PASSION IS NOT
ALWAYS LOVE

Solomon becomes most persuasive in this final lusty appeal to the girl from Shunem. In the intensity of his approach, he speaks in such a way that he exposes himself. Behind him looms the spectre of Satan who used him to do evil in the sight of God.

Solomon wrote his own confession of the intense evils in his life, and of the heartbreak they caused: "I said in mine heart, Go to now, I will prove thee with mirth; therefore enjoy pleasure . . . I sought in mine heart to give myself unto wine, yet acquainting mine heart with wisdom, and to lay hold on folly, till I might see what was good for the sons of men . . . and whatsoever mine eyes desired I kept not from them, I withheld not mine heart from any joy" (Ecclesiastes 2:1, 3, 10). These excesses brought no joy to Solomon, but

179

rather grief and remorse. "As it happeneth to the
fool, so it happeneth even to me," he wrote,
"therefore I hated life" (Ecclesiastes 2:15, 17).

In his despair, he came to several conclusions
about God which he put on record for all to read.
He wrote, "For God giveth to a man that is good
in his sight wisdom, and knowledge, and joy: but
to the sinner he giveth travail." (Ecclesiastes
2:26). He seemed to have a very strong sense of
God's ability to deal with sin, judging it if necessary. "God requireth that which is past," he wrote
in Ecclesiastes 3:15. Later he advised others:
"when thou vowest a vow unto God, defer not to
pay it; for he hath no pleasure in fools" (Ecclesiastes 5:4). Towards the end of Ecclesiastes, he
sounds the same note again: "God shall bring every work into judgment, with every secret thing,
whether it be good, or whether it be evil (Ecclesiastes 12:14)."

The hollow echo of regret is heard in the
Spirit breathed conclusions of the king. God faith-
fully records Solomon's strengths and his weaknesses: strengths that show God reaching for his
life, and weaknesses that reveal the fingerprints of
Satan.

Like the strokes of an artist putting together
the composite drawing of a criminal from the ac-
counts of eye-witnesses, each statement of Solomon shows a facet of the personality of Satan.

*"How beautiful are thy feet with shoes, O
prince's daughter! the joints of thy thighs
are like jewels, the work of the hands of a
cunning workman"* (Song of Solomon 7:1)

Both times when the shepherd gave a lengthy account of his love, he commenced at the head of the Shulamite. Solomon begins at her feet. Satan exerted his full strength to cause Messiah to fall, in fulfilment of an ancient prophecy: "thou shalt bruise his heel" (Genesis 3:15); but he failed. The whole demonic world still strives to trip the Christian.

Solomon's objective was to stumble the Shulamite; to make her fall from her high stand of purity, loyalty, and loving devotion to her shepherd.

It is very possible that the Shulamite had gone barefoot much of her life. From this she would graduate to flimsy sandals. Shoes would be the ultimate; so Solomon offered shoes. He wanted to put in her heart a desire that had nothing to do with the shepherd.

He then applied the seductive device of self-improvement. He offered her the opportunity to be clad in the best shoes; shoes that a prince's daughter would wear. The shepherd loved her as she was, but Solomon wanted to change her. The real change he was moving toward was the corruption of all the qualities that made her unique.

An entirely new situation was created when he mentioned the beauty of her feet in shoes. She had not been thinking about this. To the many appeals to her vanity, this new idea was added, just as Satan puts sin into the Christian's heart.

Judas fell because Satan put sin into his heart. John tells us, "And supper being ended, the devil having now put into the heart of Judas Iscariot, Simon's son, to betray him . . ." (John 13:2). Judas had made a deal with the chief priests to betray Jesus for money. Satan had given the concept to the traitor.

Can this happen to Christians? Indeed it can! Ananias and Sapphira were part of the newly formed church in Jerusalem. At this time, many of the Christians were selling their homes and farms to pay for spreading the gospel across the ancient world. Ananias and Sapphira sold some real estate. They agreed together to keep part of the price and to give some of it to the Lord. It was their money. Nothing was wrong with this decision.

Then they agreed to tell the church leaders that their donation was the full price. This was wrong! It was sin in the eyes of God. It caused them to lose their lives. The whole idea came from Satan. Peter said at the time: "Why hath Satan filled thine heart to lie to the Holy Ghost, and to keep back part of the price of the land? Whiles it remained, was it not thine own? and after it was sold, was it not in thine own power? Why hast thou conceived this thing in thine heart? thou hast not lied unto men, but unto God" (Acts 5:3-4).

It could be objected that it would be no sin for the Shulamite to wear shoes. This is true. Solomon was trying to create a desire in her that would make him necessary to her. It was a subtle form of seduction.

He immediately follows by calling her "prince's daughter." She was not a prince's daughter, but she knew that if she accepted Solomon's proposition she would be treated like a prince's daughter. She would have all the advantages of a prince's daughter. He had planted another concept in her heart.

The sensuous king next speaks of "the joints

of thy thighs." Apart from an act of personal force which is not suggested in the Song, Solomon had only seen the Shulamite fully clothed. Her private beauty she has in reserve for the shepherd. In a materialistic way, Solomon compares this with a jewel; beautiful to see, precious to possess.

He describes the symmetry and perfection of her body as "the work of the hands of a cunning workman." Our minds flash to the workshop of a master sculptor. We see him shaping his master-piece—every curve and line just right! He stands back, examines every detail, and smiles with satis-faction. The body is perfect.

But wait! This is so hollow and superficial. God created the body Solomon is praising, not man. The king has left God out of it, or at best has reduced Him to the stature of a talented artist. It is the life in her body that makes her physical fea-tures attractive. The most beautiful corpse has no appeal. It is beauty without God that Solomon is eulogizing.

Lucifer, the most beautiful of all angels, be-came Satan after he sinned. He is still referred to as Lucifer by many of his followers in Satanist groups, who claim to communicate with him and to receive instructions from him.

His beauty was so great that he was called "Son of the morning." When Ezekiel describes him as the ultimate angel—"Thou sealest up the sum, full of wisdom, and perfect in beauty" (Ezekiel 28:12)—It was a beauty that was created to bring God glory he was speaking about. God denounced Satan for his proud words, and pro-nounced a most unusual judgment upon him. "I will bring thee to ashes upon the earth" (Ezekiel

28:18). The Lord, who promised to give His
servants beauty for the ashes of a burned out life
of obedience to Him, will bring the corrupted
beauty of Lucifer to ashes. Beauty without God
becomes ugly. I wonder what Satan looks like now!

> *"Thy navel is like a round goblet, which*
> *wanteth not liquor: thy belly is like an*
> *heap of wheat set about with lilies: Thy*
> *two breasts are like two young roes that*
> *are twins"*   (Song of Solomon 7:2-3).

The king mingles the carnal with the spiritual
easily in his conversation. He knows well the prac-
tises of God's people, yet as a drinking man, he
could speak as freely of the delights of wine and
liquor.

This is a speech with seduction as its intent.
We find in it the ingredients of all Satanic seduction: "the lust of the flesh, and the lust of the eyes,
and the pride of life" (1 John 2:16).

The flesh lusts for what feels good without regard to morality. Though too much strong drink
makes a person drunk, a goblet of liquor gives the
good feeling, the euphoria of the social drinker. No
doubt many young women had been wooed and
won by similar sophisticated words, as Solomon
told them that they stimulated the king. He was a
master at this.

Lust of the eyes is the intense longing for
what the eye sees without moral control; sinning by
looking. "Your belly"—is compared to a heap of
wheat ornamented with lilies. It was a custom of
the time that when harvested wheat was tithed, the
Levites' portion was decorated with wild flowers of

the field. This was a gift; practical, yet beautiful. As the king saw it, the only thing the Shulamite could give him was her body. He had everything else. This delightful gift was hers to give. She could so easily give it to him. His eyes desired it.

His goal was to make her beautiful in her own eyes so that she would consider herself a gift worthy of a king.

The pride of life tries to invade every nook and cranny of our lives. We can be proud of our successes in business, with our families, or in spiritual service. We can even be proud of how humble we feel about things. Nothing is safe from this scourge unless it is placed in our Beloved's hands.

Solomon quotes the shepherd. We have no way of knowing whether he made up the expression, whether a spy had reported the words of the shepherd to the king, or whether it was a frequently used love phrase among shepherds which he appropriated. What is important to us is that he adds a new dimension; "thy breasts shall be ..." He had in mind a corrupting change for her if he could ever reach her.

The earliest recorded words of Satan to man were, "Hath God said ..." (Genesis 3:1) It was followed by a promised change, "Ye shall be as gods" (Genesis 3:5), which sounded good to Eve, although it simply meant she would know about evil.

We ought not to be surprised that Solomon used the same words as the shepherd. "Satan himself is transformed into an angel of light," the Bible teaches, (2 Corinthians 11:14). He is never more angelic than when quoting Scripture. It is not unlikely that Satan has the entire Bible committed to memory. He has had plenty of time. He certainly found the verses easily when tempting the Saviour.

> *"Thy neck is as a tower of ivory; thine eyes like the fish-pools in Heshbon, by the gate of Bath-rabbim: thy nose is as the tower of Lebanon which looketh toward Damascus: Thine head upon thee is like Carmel, and the hair of thine head like purple: the king is held in the galleries. How fair and how pleasant art thou, O love, for delights!"* (Song of Solomon 7:4-6).

When Satan tempted the Lord Jesus Christ in the wilderness, three accents were clearly made in the temptation; the accent on material things, the accent on power, and the accent on personal worth. The attempt to stumble the Saviour was a failure, but Lucifer still uses the same approach. It is seen clearly in Solomon's words to the Shulamite.

His description of her is like a geography lesson. Definite places with attractive physical features are involved. Bath-Rabbim was a gate of Heshbon where two beautiful pools existed. The tower of Lebanon facing Damascus she may have seen. Damascus had a mystique about it, not unlike Paris in our day. Mount Carmel was on the Mediterranean coast due west of the Sea of Galilee. Its silhouette was admired and enjoyed by sailors aboard ship. An ivory tower had to be imagined. Materialism shines through the words. Each is the biggest, the best, the most appealing.

He then compares her hair to purple. He was

off on colour, but the purple dye extracted from a
marine mallusk was used to colour the most costly
cloth. It was the colour of kings. The Summerian
civilization forbad common people to wear it, and
punished offenders. The king could imagine the soft
luxurious feeling of her hair, akin to the texture of
so many of the rich cloths he had handled. Again
the emphasis is on material things, just as when the
tempter requested that the Lord make bread out of
stones lying on the ground.

Satan had promised the Lord that all of the
kingdoms of the earth would be His if He would
but reverence the tempter. His power would be
boundless. It seemed like a great offer.

Solomon saw himself as the greatest king,
proud as Satan. Therefore, the greatest power the
Shulamite could have was the power over the su-
per-king. To put this into words was awkward, so
he spoke of himself as being held captive by the
tresses of her hair. This power over him was hers
he implied, she should use it.

Satan encouraged the Lord Jesus Christ to
throw Himself from the pinnacle of the temple. He
knew that the angels would not allow Him to hit
the earth, since God had given them charge to care
for Him. This test was to stand as proof that He
was Son of God. It was to be a declaration of His
personal worth.

Solomon applies the same technique to the
Shulamite. There is an inner need in most women
that makes it important to appeal to some man,
and to be able to satisfy the deep sexual drives that
are part of being a man. He tells her that she is
just right for love, but he tips his hand by using
the word "delights." This refers to the ultimate in

luxury, the best, and is used by Solomon when he confesses to his evil excesses: "I gat me men singers and women singers, and the delights of the sons of men ..." (Ecclesiastes 2:8). It was not a lifetime of love he offered, but an exciting plunge into lust-filled sex, to be followed by emptiness for her, and another new conquest for him.

It was at this point that the roar of the lion begins to be heard behind the gentle words. Peter puts the case clearly in his first epistle: "Your adversary the devil, as a roaring lion, walketh about, seeking whom he may devour: whom resist ..." (1 Peter 5:8-9). Listen to the roar of the lion in the following Scripture.

> *"This thy stature is like to a palm tree, and thy breasts to clusters of grapes. I said, I will go up to the palm tree, I will take hold of the boughs thereof: now also thy breasts shall be as clusters of the vine, and the smell of thy nose like apples; and the roof of thy mouth like the best wine for my beloved, that goeth down sweetly, causing the lips of those that are asleep to speak"* (Song of Solomon 7:7-9).

So much is said these days about the power of thinking positively that our generation almost feels that they invented positive thinking. Solomon must have been one of the great positive thinkers of all time. In this flash-back, he reveals the thoughts that ran through his mind when he first saw the beautiful Shulamite.

She was erect and stately as a palm tree. Her perfectly formed body stimulated his creative mind to think of clusters of grapes, just ready to be picked. He said to himself in essence, "This is for me! I will be the one to enjoy this girl."

Behind the real-life story of the king, we see Satan as he looks over new converts, who now desire to please their Saviour. Paul, like every faithful preacher, said that he cared for his converts, "that I may present you as a chaste virgin to Christ" (2 Corinthians 11:2). Satan purposes to defile them; to sift them as wheat as he tried with Peter, stealing away the best, and leaving only chaff.

"The serpent beguiled Eve," says Paul. He knew that the early Christians were in grave danger from the same serpent who wished to so confuse them that they would be "corrupted from the simplicity that is in Christ" (2 Corinthians 11:3).

It is likely that Solomon planned to use the most exquisite wine to accomplish the seduction. His wine would be easy to take. It would go down sweetly. Before long she would be completely under his control. Like a person speaking through the mist of sleep, she would no longer be able to resist him. She would begin saying the responses he wanted to hear.

This was a cunning plan probably used many times with complete success by the pleasure seeking king. This time, it was a total failure. The Shulamite was saved because there was a complete love in her life. She had no desires that this love would not satisfy.

Human love is not always like this, but the love of the Lord Jesus always fills the cup full. Paul knew this. That is why he prayed for the

Ephesian Christians that they would be "rooted and grounded in love" (Ephesians 3:17). He wanted them to fully understand the "love of Christ, which passeth knowledge ..." (Ephesians 3:19). This would be their great strength in the hour of extreme temptation.

The Shulamite had a trusting love. Not once in the Song does she suggest that the shepherd might fail her. "But let us, who are of the day, be sober, putting on the breastplate of faith and love" (1 Thessalonians 5:8). It is this same trusting love we need to protect us from the enemy. Our greatest danger is in the area of the heart.

Chapter 17

WALK TOGETHER
THE WHOLE WAY

At this pivotal point in the Song, returning to the Lord, and returning with the Lord are clearly taught and differentiated. It feels like a glorious victory when the Christian declares himself the Lord's possession during a moment of conviction. He has returned to the Lord! This is only the beginning. He must now return with the Lord, to complete whatever was interrupted by the departure and temptation.

"I am my beloved's, and his desire is toward me" (Song of Solomon 7:10).

In this final of three similar, but very different statements, the Shulamite pledges herself to the shepherd. There is growth in the three parallel pronouncements. To begin with, she was involved with what she had that made her secure in the shepherd's love: "My beloved is mine, and I am his." The fact that she claimed to be his becomes weak because she could be with him, but chooses to remain by herself.

The second time, she puts the shepherd first, finding joy in the fact that she did belong to him, and that was the way she now willed it to be. "I am my beloved's, and my beloved is mine." There is increased credibility in her words because she knows where he is and immediately goes to him.

Now she finds her joy in his response, "His desire is toward me." In direct contrast to the many love affairs of the licentious Solomon, the shepherd loved only her. She was the whole focus of his desire, and he desired her with his whole being. There is a hidden note that suggests that now this desire of his will have fulfilment. She is now responding. Their mutual love is now accompanied with mutual responsiveness.

The Christian who claims to love the Lord, but has no actions to give evidence of that love builds a poor case before a doubting world. The Lord Himself puts the matter straight. "If a man love me, he will keep my words" (John 14:23). He places no value on the form of love that does not motivate a Christian to read the Bible, to respond with obedience to God's will, or to pray about the events of the day lived for Him. He is right down at our level when He speaks of our response.

The Shulamite seems to have a suppressed excitement in her words, as though she is really saying, "His desire is still towards me . . ." After her rejection and compromise she can hardly be-

lieve it. We know the feeling. When we return to
the Lord we are most aware of our own emptiness,
but He is willing to receive. He taught His disciples to forgive a brother seventy times seven times
so that we would understand that there is infinity
in His willingness to forgive, to receive and to keep
on loving.

She has now returned to her beloved with a
declaration of her will. Now let us consider where
she goes as she returns with him to the place and
action of his choice.

> *"Come, my beloved, let us go forth into
> the field; let us lodge in the villages"*
> (Song of Solomon 7:11).

The Shulamite is still speaking, but now she is
speaking of the shepherd's desires. Twice before he
has used the invitation word "Come," expressing
his wish that they might return home. Now she
completely concurs. She uses the same word with
the same meaning.

We begin to return with the Lord when we begin to use His Word with the same intent that He
had in writing and speaking it in the first place.

The fields and villages were the natural environment of the shepherd. He belonged in the rural
setting. The sophistication of the court put him at
a disadvantage. We return with the Lord when we
frequent the places where He belongs. There is a
link between having fellowship with Him and having fellowship with others who love Him. "Not for-
saking the assembling of ourselves together" (Hebrews 10:25), means that we do not reject participation in Church functions where the Lord and

His Word are central. We will be careful to avoid palace-like religious settings, where the power of Scripture is minimized, and where the Lord Jesus is seen as remote from human society and its needs.

The shepherd would not ever have left the fields and villages had it not been for the Shulamite. He left them to search for her, hoping to bring her back by the force of his love. Her words, "Let us go," were the echo of all that he had been working for during the whole happening. The Lord desires our fellowship so much that He "died for us, that, whether we wake or sleep, we should live together with him" (1 Thessalonians 5:10). Our part is simply to let Him. He will not force His will upon us.

"Let us get up early to the vineyards; let us see if the vine flourish, whether the tender grape appear, and the pomegranates bud forth: there will I give thee my loves. The mandrakes give a smell, and at our gates are all manner of pleasant fruits, new and old, which I have laid up for thee, O my beloved" (Song of Solomon 7:12-13).

When a Christian dedicates, surrenders, or yields his life to the Lord, he is really saying that his life and the life of the risen Christ have not been moving together. He now submits to the omnipotent Beloved so that Divine power will enable him to accomplish what has been impossible for him to do by himself. The divergent lines of movement of the two lives come together, and the Christian purposes in his heart that they will go on together from that moment.

For this to come true, there will need to be a merging of the interests that have up to this time been different.

The Shulamite has been interested in the court of Solomon, in the little foxes, in the summer house. These were not the shepherd's interests, nor would they become his interests. To walk with him again, she must become interested in the things that make up his life, as she had been before.

This shows as she mentions getting early to the vineyards, being concerned whether the vines flourished, watching for the pomegranates to bud. These things had made up her life with him before. She is now returning with him.

"There will I give thee my loves," she says. The word she uses—"loves"—can mean either love tokens, or loved persons according to Strong's Concordance. She now focuses her love on him as a person. She has tokens of her love to give him. She goes on to tell him what they are.

One of the love tokens was mandrakes, very likely planted by the Shulamite at the family home for the enjoyment of the shepherd. The girl is a very uncomplicated person by our standards, and planting something specially for her lover would be within the likelihood of her culture. The mandrake had small fruit, often called the love-apple and had a potato-like root of unusual shape. They appear to have had a characteristic fragrance appealing to the shepherd.

Other fruits had been picked by this domesticated girl because she knew they would please him. They had been chosen over a lengthy period of time. Some may have been preserved, to be brought with her into her new home. They were picked for him, that he might enjoy them with her. That is what made them love-tokens.

The fruits were precious for two reasons. They had been "laid up" for the shepherd, and they were the fruits that would give him satisfaction.

There ought to be in our lives a fragrance that has grown because we cultivated it for the Lord we profess to love. There should also be fruit that He desires, which we have brought so that He could enjoy it. These will be precious evidences of our love to Him. We will both enjoy them as we move along together.

In the New Testament the sweet fragrance is mentioned in regards to two services which we can render to the Lord: witnessing about Him, and supporting others who witness with our financial resources. A savour which Christ delights in surrounds our lives as we tell others of Him. As we dig into our personal funds to support the work of evangelism and church building, whether at home or abroad, He enjoys that same sweet savour.

Fruit is linked with the work of the Holy Spirit in our lives; with lives we have influenced for our Beloved; with the lives we live that give evidence that we have repented; with the good works we do because we believe; and with the words of praise and worship we offer to the Lord. These fruits are most precious to the Lord, but we must lay them up for Him. They will not just happen. They will be the outgrowth of our real love for the Lord Jesus Christ, and of our desire to please and honour Him.

"Oh that thou wert as my brother, that sucked the breasts of my mother! when I

*should find thee without, I would kiss
thee; yea, I should not be despised. I
would lead thee, and bring thee into my
mother's house, who would instruct me: I
would cause thee to drink of spiced wine
of the juice of my pomegranate"*

(Song of Solomon 8:1-2).

The wish of the Shulamite is really a yearning
for greater closeness than the eastern betrothal al-
lows. She did not want the shepherd for a brother:
she wanted him for a husband. Brother and sister
would have found it easier to travel through the
fields and villages without offending the mores of
the day. She could have kissed her brother in pub-
lic, could have led him by his hand. Closeness
would not have been a problem.

As betrothed people, they were liable to be
despised by any contradiction of custom.

The echo of these words is heard every time a
Christian says, "I want so much to be close to the
Lord, if only some circumstance were changed so
that I might truly embrace Him." This is just as
unreal as the Shulamite's wish. If it ever was granted, the fulfilment would be more problem than
help. It is true love, working harmony whatever
the circumstances, that makes our life with Him
come together.

She wanted to be able to do four things: find
him, kiss him, bring him inside so that he could instruct her, for that is the construction of the
words, and refresh him with something she had
made.

Wishing will not bring the spiritual counterpart of these four desires to us. They must be

claimed. They must be cherished, if our living fellowship with Christ is to be the adventure He planned.

We need to find Him and never leave His fellowship ever again. Does He seem distant to you? The Bible promise comes from His own lips: "Ye shall seek me, and find me, when ye shall search for me with all your heart" (Jeremiah 29:13). Many do lip service to the Lord Jesus Christ, but the person finds Him who searches with his heart.

"Kiss the Son" (Psalm 2:12), the psalmist says. "I would kiss thee," we hear from the Shulamite. The Lord misses the full embrace of our love much of the time. We hear Him say to us as He did long ago, "Thou gavest me no kiss" (Luke 7:45). There is commitment in a kiss between lovers. The Lord looks for this commitment from those who claim to love Him.

The Shulamite had gone to the court of Solomon from her mother's house, her home until marriage. Her submissive heart now desires to hear the shepherd tell her his plans and hopes. She wants to take him into her mother's house for the instruction. If we have been out of touch with the Lord, our future spiritual growth will depend on our returning to the place of departure. Returning with Him involves coming to the place where we first missed our footing.

A very apt illustration of this is seen in the movements of Abram. Abram built an altar between Bethel and Hai before his departure to Egypt where he had extreme problems. He returned from Egypt and his course is charted in Scripture: "And he went on his journeys from the south even to Bethel, unto the place where his tent

had been at the beginning, between Bethel and
Hai; unto the place of the altar, which he made
there at the first: and there Abram called on the
name of the Lord" (Genesis 13:3-4). It seems as
if he had come to the place of this altar, before
he could go to new experiences with the Lord.

Finally, the Shulamite desired to give the
shepherd special things to refresh and bless him.
She knew that this would give him joy in which
she could share. The drink she wanted to give him
seems to have been her personal recipe, something
she could make well. This is how we should see our
gifts. We have been equipped by God to do certain
things well. We should see in these special opportu-
nities to bless and refresh our Beloved.

> *"His left hand should be under my head,*
> *and his right hand should embrace me. I*
> *charge you, O daughters of Jerusalem,*
> *that ye stir not up, nor awake my love,*
> *until he please"*
>
> (Song of Solomon 8:3-4).

She is now leaving the daughters of Jerusalem.
They have watched the Shulamite, often in wonder, sometimes perplexed, sometimes admiring.
They have never doubted that she loved the shepherd, but they saw Solomon's offer as a powerful
influence in her life. She was human, often more
emotionally impelled than rationally controlled.

She reminds them of her words spoken at the
time of the struggle. She had told them at that
time how it had been—how she had loved the shepherd and had shared his tender embrace. It had

seemed gone forever then, as if there was no way back.

Now she has made her choice. Her life would be dove-tailed with the shepherd's. Never again would she be swayed by a false lover. Through the experience of separation, she now knew how great a part his love played in her life, and how dependent her happiness was upon it.

The Lord should have the right to love the Christian, and to be loved in return. We should be responsive to His touch. It is on the level of faith, but should be no less real because of that. Peter saw the Lord physically, but it was after the Lord had returned to heaven that Peter wrote: "Whom having not seen, ye love; in whom, though now ye see him not, yet believing, ye rejoice with joy unspeakable and full of glory" (1 Peter 1:8).

The marginal reading of the adjuration is, "Why should ye stir up, or why should ye awake love?" The Shulamite is asking the daughters of Jerusalem why they should ever stir up love to Solomon in any maid, to rob her of the joy she herself is now entering. It is a reasonable question. They have nothing to gain by this behaviour. Much human activity, influenced by Satan, has no rational explanation.

No snatches of conversation are shared with us until the two lovers are almost home. The journey of over forty miles appears to have been made on foot. When Solomon made the trip, he had been attended by sixty valiant men, "because of fear in the night," as he travelled in his car of state. The couple walked without protection. No fear grips the Shulamite. She trusts the shepherd to see her safely home.

*"Who is this that cometh up from the
wilderness, leaning upon her beloved?"*
(Song of Solomon 8:5).

The villagers spot them in the distance. By
this time, the Shulamite feels the weariness of so
long a trip. She likely has sore feet. She leans on
the shepherd as she walks. They are coming home
from the wilderness to the place where they love to
be together.

*"I raised thee up under the apple tree:
there thy mother brought thee forth; there
she brought thee forth that bare thee"*
(Song of Solomon 8:5).

They are now on familiar ground. They pass
an apple tree full of memories. The shepherd reminds her that this is the place where she was first
moved with love toward him. This is where he had
won her heart. It was also the place where they
pledged themselves to each other in eastern betrothal. No father was in the picture. The mother
pledged the Shulamite. It was a very special place
to both of them.

There is always a preciousness about the place
where our Christian life began. It strikes a special
note in the heart to remember the wonderful simplicity of it. Recently, I drove by the tiny house
where my mother led me to the Lord. I felt a
subdued excitement to be there again, where God
had worked the miracle of imparting eternal life
to a little child.

The same is true of the place where we gave
back to Him the life He died to save, that He might

possess it, and pour His love through it. "Present your bodies," says Paul (Romans 12:1), but it is so much more than this. It is the surrender of a stubborn will; the yielding of a carnal spirit; the opening of a blockaded heart; and the spilling over of a soul that is learning to love. When we have done this, and then slip back into indecisive half-loving, the return to Him must include the return with Him to the commitment of the past, so that the future can be the life together He died to give us in the first place.

Chapter 18

THOSE VOWS
MEAN SOMETHING

No description is found in the Song to tell of the rustic wedding of the Shulamite and her shepherd beloved. The only part of the ceremony shared with us is the vows of love which they made with each other. These vows were very precious to them because they contained the sum total of the wisdom their combined experience had gathered.

They speak the words with commitment in their hearts, and this is the only way to make a vow. To many couples standing before God, the vows are spoken with neither conviction nor commitment, and the wear and tear of life soon erodes the good intentions they felt in the flush of romantic love.

A vow is a contract, a binding pledge, a solemn promise, which has no relationship to how much worse or better things may become than at the time the vow is made. Lovers merge their lives with the vows they take before the Lord, and the two become one flesh. The person who makes a vow or covenant with the Lord merges his life with the Lord's. He commits himself to walk with the Divine Lover for the fulfilment of his commitment.

The Lord makes it plain that we should yield to His control, and that He sees this as a binding commitment: "Know ye not, that to whom ye yield yourselves servants to obey, his servants ye are" (Romans 6:16). The act of yielding our redeemed bodies to the Lord for His use is a must if He is to use us as channels for His love and truth. This is why the Holy Spirit pleads through Paul for us to present our bodies. It is only when we do this that we may prove "what is that good, and acceptable, and perfect will of God" (Romans 12:2). We can choose to live the Christian life without this commitment if we want to, but this means that we will never know the great plan that the Master Designer mapped out to please and to fulfil us.

Since wedding vows are the equal responsibility of both bride and groom, consider first what the shepherd, representing our Beloved meant when he spoke the words.

"Set me as a seal upon thine heart, as a seal upon thine arm" (Song of Solomon 8:6).

The seal of love is a person. The shepherd wanted the Shulamite to have him in possession of her heart so that it would be sealed to all others. The evidence of this would be seen in things she did. Her arms would be active in things that were pleasing to her bridegroom, but would be sealed, closed off from activities that would hurt or disappoint him. It was a simple vow, but right to the point.

As the Lord Jesus whispers these same words to us, we realize that our commitment to Him means that our hearts are sealed by Him from all others. When our love enthrones Him, He will guard the surrendered heart. The battle with sin is no longer a struggle. We just claim the victory He has won.

The evidence that we have allowed Him to seal our hearts is that His seal is on our arms. Work for Him is no longer tedious. It is now the labour of love He said it would be. He sees the seal on our heart. The world sees the seal on our arm. It is Christ in my heart that gives the powerful witness of Christ in my life.

The Shulamite echoes the shepherd's words. She hardly needs to say them, there has been such an abundance of evidence. She knows she is the seal of his heart. The whole Song portrays his thoughts of her. The seal of love on his arm is seen in the acts of love and strength which he has done, with her good as his only motivation.

The Lord Jesus loved us like this. The seal of love is on His heart, for He said: "As the Father hath loved me, so have I loved you" (John 15:9). This is love at its peak—the love of God the Father for God the Son—so great that the Father would let Him come: so overwhelming that He would come.

The seal of His love is still on His arms. The marks of the Calvary death will forever tell us that from eternity He loved us in time. His love is eternal. There will be no change in it.

*"Love is strong as death; jealousy is cruel
as the grave: the coals thereof are coals
of fire, which hath a most vehement
flame"*   (Song of Solomon 8:6).

The strength of love now occupies the words
of the vow. Again the shepherd speaks. He tells of
the measure of his love: "strong as death." He
would have died for the Shulamite had that been
necessary. There is a natural jealousy in love like
this; jealousy that protects and guards; that saves
and retrieves. The fire of that jealousy that cares
burns in the shepherd's heart like a flame that
would not go out, even when rejection seemed im-
minent.

Now hear the Lord Jesus saying these words.
His love is as strong as His death, but what a death
that was; "even the death of the cross" (Philippians 2:8). Jesus arrived at Golgotha with the
dried remains of the blood sweat of Gethsemane
still on His face. His body was stained with blood,
and with the forming clots of a whipping with the
scourge. A crown, woven from long thorns, was
crushed down on His head piercing into the tender
tissue around His eyes and temples.

The soldiers threw Him roughly on to the
cross, hammered crude nails through His hands and
feet, then with brute-force stood it up on end to
drop it without mercy into the prepared post-hole.
"All my bones are out of joint," He groaned
(Psalm 22:14). He hung in the blazing sun,
parched with thirst, struggling for every breath
while His enemies stood and watched in scorn. They
mocked his prayers, joked, and taunted Him about

His sufferings, still scoffing His claim to Divine titles.

Three long hours passed like this. Then in mid-afternoon an eerie darkness settled over Calvary. In the darkness, God the Judge punished God the Sinbearer for the sins of the human race, as though the sinless Jesus had committed every sin of man. "He hath poured out his soul unto death," Isaiah exclaims (Isaiah 53:12). We hear the man on the centre cross pierce the darkness to tell us that He is in a terror of agony. "My God, my God, why hast thou forsaken me?" He says.

The darkness lifts. He calls out, "It is finished!" There is a stillness among the onlookers as they fix their eyes on the huddled figure hanging crucified. Swollen, distorted, torn and discoloured, He hardly resembles a man. In shocked horror, they know that even the vicious torture of a cross could not do this to Him. "Many were astonished," Isaiah records, "his visage was so marred more than any man, and his form more than the sons of men" (Isaiah 52:14). One of the Romans gasped, "Truly this man was the Son of God" (Mark 15:39).

It was a great death: great in that it was God who died; great because it was payment in full for our salvation; great because it points out the enormity of human sin, while providing a basis for God's forgiveness of our sins. His love, as great as His death, is great, great love.

There is a burning jealousy in the heart of the Lord Jesus that Satan, from whom He delivered us, should never get his hands on us again. All of the cruelty of our Beloved's death had its source in Satan. He planted the sinful lusts in the heart of

Jesus' murderers. He hates the Christian as he hates Christ. The Lord is jealous over us with His protecting, caring, supporting jealousy—the jealousy that burns within Him to help and guard us.

This jealousy burns with "a most vehement flame." Clarke explains that this is really a "flame of Jah." The fire that burned in the heart of the shepherd is the same fire that burns in the heart of God for His people.

The bride repeats the same vows. This is where we come in. She repeats the vows to the shepherd. We repeat them to the Lord.

Our love is as strong as our death. The Beloved has asked us to reckon ourselves dead to sin, so that He might be alive within us. It is only as we are dead to sin that the holy Son of God can walk with us, and be at home in the lives we are living. If we truly desire Him, we will not count this as cost. Our love is as strong as our death.

Jealousy comes in as we guard that which is the Lord's, so that He alone might have it. Our thoughts are brought into captivity to Him. Our bodies are His alone. Our time is redeemed that He might have it all. The fire of jealousy burns for the Lord as we refuse to allow anything of us to be lost that should be His.

> "*Many waters cannot quench love, neither can the floods drown it*"
> (Song of Solomon 8:7).

The shepherd has seen the love he valued more than life almost washed away with the flood of temptation. At no point did his love falter. He understood the stability of love.

The stability of the love of Christ has not been changed by the events of the passing centuries. He loved us when we were nothing but a plan in His Creator heart. He loved us through the fall in Eden and through suffering of the cross. "The waters are come in unto my soul," He exclaimed, but this did not change His love (Psalm 69:1). We hear this vow from His lips, and know that no flood in the future will ever drown His love.

It is not so easy for us to respond with the same words about our love. The Shulamite must have trembled a little as she spoke these words, yet remembered how the waters had almost quenched her love while she was in Jerusalem. The one thing that made her strong was that she had gotten to know the shepherd, through this experience, in a way that all past familiarity had not taught her.

We are able to witness this good confession when we know the Lord well enough that we trust in His power. The enabling Lord is able to give us the ability to love Him with a stable love. The Holy Spirit floods our heart with this love. All other surging waves are controlled.

Paul understood that knowing the Lord well was the key to living for His glory. This motivated him to say: "I count all things but loss for the excellency of the knowledge of Christ Jesus my Lord" (Philippians 3:8). He wanted to win the Christ who had won him. He had discovered the great objective of Christian living. It is to know Christ intellectually, personally, intimately and responsively. He stated the way he understood that his life should move, and how this objective could be realized: "that I may know him, and the power

of his resurrection, and the fellowship of his sufferings, being made conformable unto his death"
(Philippians 3:10).

Paul speaks with authority about some of the
floods in his Roman epistle, making reference to
the absolute stability of the love of our Beloved.
"Who shall separate us from the love of Christ?
shall tribulation, or distress, or persecution, or fam-
ine, or nakedness, or peril, or sword? . . . Nay, in all
these things we are more than conquerors, through
him that loved us. For I am persuaded, that neither
death, nor life, nor angels, nor principalities, nor
powers, nor things present, nor things to come, nor
height, nor depth, nor any other creature, shall be
able to separate us from the love of God, which is in
Christ Jesus our Lord" (Romans 8:35-39). Though
nothing can separate the child of God from the
love of God, the Christian can falter in his response if he does not know the Lord intimately.
Paul thought of this as he closed his letter to the
Ephesians with that unusual salutation: "Grace be
with all them that love our Lord Jesus Christ in
sincerity" (Ephesians 6:24). This is the stability
of love that the Lord desires in us. It is included in
the vow we share with Him.

> *"If a man would give all the substance
> of his house for love, it would utterly be
> contemned"*   (Song of Solomon 8:7).

The shepherd spoke the vows they had planned together. Love meant giving himself to the
Shulamite. If he ever gave things instead of himself, she was to hold him in contempt. The Shulamite listened, remembering how the things Solomon

had offered once appealed to her, but knowing that
this was what she needed from a man.

Then she spoke. She did not have much to
give; but she knew that unless she gave herself first
of all, the gifts she could give the shepherd would
not mean much.

This is how we must relate to our Beloved.
Any gift that we might bring to Him is valueless
unless we give ourselves first. He is more interested
in us than in anything we might bring. Besides, He
already has everything. The only reason our gifts
hold any value at all is that they are the outgrowth
of a love that made us give ourselves.

The churches in Macedonia during the first
century were an exciting example for all succeeding
generations of believers. The Holy Spirit records
that they, "first gave their own selves to the Lord"
(2 Corinthians 8:5). Everything else they gave
after that was precious to the Lord. He accepted it
as an offering of love because they had first given
themselves.

We have a tendency to become preoccupied
with the benefits of trusting Christ. This is reflected in many of our hymns about heaven, happiness, joy and security. These, and all the other advantages of salvation, are only side issues, although
each has infinite value.

Our great possession is Christ! If He had
found a way to give all these things to us without
giving Himself, we would never have known the
wonder of His power to love.

The Bible tells us that He "gave himself for
our sins" (Galatians 1:4); that He, "gave himself for us" (Titus 2:14); and that He "gave himself a ransom" (1 Timothy 2:6). Peter stresses

His personal involvement as he writes: "Who his own self bare our sins in his own body on the tree. . . . by whose stripes ye were healed" (1 Peter 2:24).

After His death, He could hardly stay away from the disciples. His soul yearned to be with them. We read: "Jesus himself drew near" (Luke 24:15); "Jesus himself stood in the midst" (Luke 24:36); and "Jesus showed himself to his disciples" (John 21:14). Before leaving for the last time, He promised that His invisible presence would accompany them. He would be with them. They would have Him, not just the things that accompany salvation.

The Holy Spirit emphasizes that it is the Lord Jesus who is coming back to receive the church: "The Lord himself shall descend from heaven with a shout" (1 Thessalonians 4:16). This is the vow He made to His disciples: "If I go and prepare a place for you, I will come again, and receive you unto myself; that where I am, there ye may be also" (John 14:3). There is no substitute for our Beloved. He does not ever intend to offer one.

Chapter 19

KEEP YOUR
LOVE GROWING

The marriage is past. A soliloquy by the bride surveys her new interests. Her fulfilled vows have brought her to a new level of confidence and joy.

It is really a picture of her thought life. The words reflect the thoughts that drift through her mind, as well as her responses. Her new life-style is in focus since what she thinks moulds and shapes her actions.

> *"We have a little sister, and she hath no breasts: what shall we do for our sister in the day when she shall be spoken for? If she be a wall, we will build upon her a palace of silver; and if she be a door, we will inclose her with boards of cedar"*
> (Song of Solomon 8:8-9).

Through the union of marriage, the little girl, sister of either the Shulamite or the shepherd, now becomes the sister of both. She had been the sister of one or the other of them, but not both of them.

She is a little sister, not yet showing the physical development of maturity. From her own experience, the Shulamite knows that her sister will need guidance later on, when the suitors come to ask for her hand.

The Shulamite had gained much understanding about helping others from the shepherd's tender care towards her. He had known what she was like. If he had angrily demanded her return with him, he likely would have lost her. He had understood her needs, and had sought to meet them, not forcing her to be someone other than she was. Rather, he brought out of her the commitment to real love that had brought them together in the first place.

In her heart she resolved to watch over the little sister with love. "If she be a wall . . . If she be a door . . ." The Shulamite was purposing to watch the areas of the little sister's development, so that she could help her to a maturity that would be right for her.

A wall is a plain structure. Build a palace of silver on it, and the serviceable structure becomes an edifice of beauty. A door is just an assortment of pieces of wood until it is framed. Enclose it with boards of durable cedar, and the door will function effectively for many years.

She wanted to bring out the potential beauty and purpose in the little sister's life. Her one objective was to help the little girl find her place in life, so that ultimately she would enjoy the same love

the Shulamite had found. She had no doubt that
the shepherd would work together with her in this.
It would be the spillover of their love for each
other.

The overflow of the Christian's love for the
Lord stirs him to disciple others. Discipling is not
just influencing another Christian to be a duplicate
of the discipler, developing similar gifts and engaging in the same practices and activities. The discipler learns to work within the framework of the
young believer's abilities, interests and responses.
He must bring him first of all into an intimate and
personal relationship with the Lord. When the disciple develops to that point, the seductive forces of
Satan will pull vigorously against him. He will then
need continuous example, encouragement, help, and
love, until his interests merge with the Lover of his
soul, and his Spirit-given gifts begin to show.

The Lord wants us to teach others. The American Standard Version translates His commission—
"Make disciples" (Matthew 28:19). When the
young Christian becomes a disciple, he should immediately desire to disciple others. This is the cyclic
plan of our Lord. He began it. His own twelve disciples continued the approach. It has often been interrupted by Christians who failed to see how it
should work. There is great hazard for the church
that makes converts without making disciples.

There are four distinct phases to the cycle of
discipling. Firstly, you as a disciple must yield
completely to the Lord's control, with all resistance
to His love and direction gone. Secondly, the example of your life must draw from another Christian the desire to walk before the Lord like you.
Thirdly, you must build into the other's heart a

commitment to obey the Lord, and to yield to Him. Fourthly, your teaching must apply Divine principles to daily life, so that the disciple will know how to live for the Lord in today's world.

The fourth phase is the most neglected because it requires the greatest time and effort. There is no theory in it, but rather the grit and grind of living Christ in a world that is against Christ. It requires much fellowship between disciple and discipler, selflessness on the part of both, witness of ministry in action, as well as participation by the disciple. There will need to be demonstration of the power of God. Spiritual vision must be built. Work must be delegated. Faith must grow because the discipler has faith. The mature disciple emerges. He has already walked through fatigue, exhaustion, disappointment, as well as exhilaration, joy, fruitful times of praise, and great victories over Satan, with the discipler.

Down through the centuries, great stress has been placed on Proverbs 22:6 as the basis for child rearing. "Train up a child in the way he should go: and when he is old, he will not depart from it." Faithful parents have often quoted these words in bewildered dismay when a well instructed child has turned aside from the faith. The English revisers put a footnote to this verse which may help us to understand its application a little better. They suggest that it should be: "Train up a child according to his way . . ." This makes allowance for the natural bent of the child, without taking away the need for training.

The father with a great knowledge of Scripture may have a child with an I.Q. of 80. There is no way that the child's mind can function like the father's, but this need not be a disappointment. The child can still be trained in the things of God. There will be a ministry for him if he is well instructed about the Lord, as long as the father does not try to make a rubber stamp of himself in his child.

Faith in Christ, and surrender to Him, is within the range of life on every level of intellectual accomplishment, emotional growth, or social agility. We only lose when we try to bend a life into a shape which it cannot hold, and teach that this is what is involved in following Jesus.

> *"I am a wall, and my breasts like towers:*
> *then was I in his eyes as one that found*
> *favour"* (Song of Solomon 8:10).

The Shulamite knew who she was. There is neither pride nor false modesty in her words. She is not even saying that it is better to be a wall than a door. It is just that she thinks of herself now as a wall. Her breasts are like the towers on a bleak wall that add to the beauty of it.

A wall had several specific functions in the day of the Shulamite. Since they were costly to build, many had to live and work without them. A wall outlined the possession of a landowner so that the world knew what was his. It protected those inside from marauders and robbers. It kept the flocks from wandering and getting lost, and thus saved the keepers much labour. It allowed freedom of action for those inside, since those outside the wall could not idly watch them as they passed.

She was a wall. Standing true to the shepherd, she told the whole world she was his. His possession in her was now safe. He no longer had to span mountains and valleys to find her. There was a strength and steadiness in her since she had taken the vows.

The towers on the wall, besides giving it character, and making it attractive, provided a distant view for those inside. Her breasts represent maturity and fruitfulness. She now had the long view of mature growth. Seductive flattery was no longer attractive. The allurements of the world's pleasure become dull when we know intimacy with the Lord.

In a momentary flashback she says, "then was I in his eyes as one that found favour." When she was not attractive, when she was not true to him, when she was immature, she was still loved. The shepherd's love had bridged the gaps she had created. His love had been steady from the moment of his first interest.

We can understand how she feels. The Lord loved us when we were defiled, guilty, rebellious, and completely unworthy of Him. The days of our past that are a nightmare for many even to remember, had no effect on His love. He kept seeing in us what He could enjoy if we would turn to Him.

> "Solomon had a vineyard at Baal-hamon;
> he let out the vineyard unto keepers;
> every one for the fruit thereof was to bring
> a thousand pieces of silver. My vineyard,
> which is mine, is before me: thou, O
> Solomon, must have a thousand, and those
> that keep the fruit thereof two hundred"
> (Song of Solomon 8:11-12).

The Shulamite uses the past tense when she mentions Solomon because he is in her past. He had a vineyard in a place now unknown which he leased to keepers. The Shulamite had learned of the financial agreement between Solomon and his workers. The sums she mentions were enormous to her—comparable to a salaried office employee speaking about a million dollars.

In comparison to the great vineyard of the king, the Shulamite's vineyard is small and insignificant. She looks after it by herself, shares some of the fruit with her husband, and possibly assists the family income by selling some of the grapes for a few pieces of silver, but it is hers! She has none of the strain of trying to meet the demands of a Solomon.

We almost feel a shiver of delight and relief run through her as she bursts out: "Thou, O Solomon, must have a thousand;" or, as the Amplified Bible renders it: "You, O Solomon, can have your thousand." It had no interest for her at all. She was glad to be rid of everything that was Solomon's.

> *"Thou that dwellest in the gardens, the companions hearken to thy voice: cause me to hear it"*   (Song of Solomon 8:13).

As she thinks again of the shepherd, the Shulamite envisions him out in the fields. The most barren field becomes a garden to her when he is there. She sees him as a leader of men. She knows that the others who are with him, tending the flocks, listen to him. Then her personal desire surfaces: "Cause me to hear it!" she exclaims.

There is nothing complicated about her thoughts, but then, even the deep things of God only become complicated when human thought patterns mix them up. God's plan is that we should live "in simplicity and godly sincerity, not with fleshly wisdom, but by the grace of God" (2 Corinthians 1:12). It is a good plan for us to follow.

In a sense, the shepherd dwells in the gardens while he works in the fields. The fields make up his gardens. Earlier in the Song, we saw how the human heart is compared to a garden. Paul prayed that Christ might "dwell" in the Christian's hearts by faith, the word "dwell" meaning to be at home. Thus, the Song concludes with the parallel of Christ, our Beloved, dwelling in our hearts.

Those who have found an emotional devotional attachment to Christ their Beloved soon find that they want to be in the field with Him. "As workers together with him" (2 Corinthians 6:1), they desire that they should hear His voice in the turmoil of intense activity, not just in the passive prayerful enjoyment of His love in the quiet place.

The companions do listen to Him. Since He is all-knowing, we may tell Him that we love Him, and He values this, but we cannot add to His store of information. It is vitally important that we keep on listening to what He has to say. This will give to us the expanding knowledge we need in every field of service.

The Shulamite, totally devoted to the shepherd, needs to continue hearing him speak both love and instruction.

Our relationship to the Lord will only remain vitally alive if we keep on listening to Him by reading, learning, even memorizing the Scriptures.

We need to put His words into our minds, and to live with these words as the daily guide and control of our behaviour.

> *"Make haste, my beloved, and be thou like to a roe or to a young hart upon the mountains of spices"*
> (Song of Solomon 8:14).

Spices each have a unique fragrance. Each can flavour a substance in which it is mixed. Spices cause a change in their environment. They do not come in mountains either. A mountain of spices has to be built by man, or else imagined.

What would a mountain of different spices be like? It would have a most unusual atmosphere. Its variety would be beyond belief. Dig into the mountain anywhere and it would contain surprises!

The prayer of the Shulamite had previously been, "that the spices thereof may flow out" (Song of Solomon 4:16). She wanted this so that the shepherd would be pleased and would come to her. It is like the prayer of a Christian that his life will become acceptable to the Lord. Now that she committed herself without reserve to him for his enjoyment and fellowship, she anticipates an increase in the spices that please him—mountains of them.

At one time she had said, "be thou like a roe or a young hart upon the mountains of Bether," wanting him to be distant, so she could please herself. Now she desires him as close as possible, as though running across mountains that are the fruit of her life, possessing, enjoying, and loving them. The word "roe" has the idea of beauty in it. "Hart" contains the thought of strength.

She portrays for us the Christian who desires that the beauty and strength of the Beloved should be seen in the life he lives; a fruitful, fragrant life that gives Him pleasure. Her love has matured, growing to the point where she has no desire to be away from him ever again.

"Make haste," she calls.

"Make haste!" we echo, calling the Beloved to enjoy, during the short years of time, the lives He died to save for eternity.

THE PIVOT FAMILY CLASSICS SERIES

INEXPENSIVE EDITIONS . . .
COMPLETE AND UNABRIDGED

☐ **ABIDE IN CHRIST** by Andrew Murray. The famous book in which the author writes about the true meaning of the words "abide in me." Introduction by William J. Petersen, editor of *Eternity* magazine. **95¢**

☐ **DAILY STRENGTH FOR DAILY NEEDS** by Mary W. Tileston. Each page, one for every day of the year, strikes a note of comfort and assurance for today, and hope and confidence for tomorrow. Treasured by countless readers for nearly a century, an endless source of insight and inspiration. **$1.25**

☐ **GOLD DUST** by Charlotte Yonge. Daily reminders of Divine love, brief but memorable restatements of the truths the heart knows but the mind may forget. A storehouse of faith and understanding for the whole family. **95¢**

☐ **IN HIS STEPS** by Charles M. Sheldon. A new edition of the most popular novel ever written, with an inspiring introduction by Donald T. Kauffman. **95¢**

☐ **IN TUNE WITH THE INFINITE** by Ralph Waldo Trine. Drawing on his inspired understanding of Scripture, the author points out the way to peace of mind, in one of the inspirational classics of all time. **$1.25**

☐ **KEPT FOR THE MASTER'S USE** by Frances Ridley Havergal. Twelve paths to participating in God's mighty promise, in a book of lasting inspiration and guidance. **95¢**

☐ **OF THE IMITATION OF CHRIST** by Thomas à Kempis. The most famous book of devotions in Christendom. Meditations on the life and teachings of Jesus and second only to the Bible as a guide and inspiration. **95¢**

☐ **THE PILGRIM'S PROGRESS** by John Bunyan. An exciting larger-than-life adventure story and a document of faith and inspiration. Introduction by Donald T. Kauffman. **95¢**

☐ **WHAT ALL THE WORLD'S A-SEEKING** by Ralph Waldo Trine. The one great principle of life and how it can be understood and used. A truly "how to" for those who will open themselves to the chance for joy and peace. **$1.25**

Buy them at your bookstore or use this handy coupon

THREE VOLUMES IN ONE...
NEVER BEFORE IN PAPERBACK

The Pivot INSPIRATION THREE LIBRARY

brings you the best of inspirational thought together in new, bargain-priced volumes for family enrichment. The larger type and convenient size, the choice of the best authors and selections, make each volume a shared adventure in wisdom and insight for young and old.

☐ **VOLUME ONE** contains *As A Man Thinketh* by James Allen; *Acres of Diamonds* by Russell Conwell; and *Essay on Self-Reliance* by Ralph Waldo Emerson. Special introduction by David Poling. **$1.25**

☐ **VOLUME TWO** contains *The Greatest Thing In The World* by Henry Drummond; *The Song Of Our Syrian Guest* by William Allen Knight; and *The Practice Of The Presence of God* by Brother Lawrence. Special introduction by David Poling. **$1.25**

☐ **VOLUME THREE** contains three original anthologies of classic-Christian thought: *The Wisdom of Martin Luther; The Wisdom of John Wesley; The Wisdom of John Calvin.* Selected and with a special introduction by David Poling. **$1.25**

☐ **VOLUME FIVE** contains three Christmas Classics: *The Story Of The Other Wise Man* by Henry Van Dyke; *A Christmas Carol* by Charles Dickens; and *A Gift Of the Magi* by O. Henry. Special introduction by David Poling. **$1.25**

Buy them at your bookstore or use this handy coupon